JN418589

Great Tales of Sound

Written by Bae, Myungjin and Kim, Myungsook

Great Tales of Sound

Written by Bae, Myungjin and Kim, Myungsook
Published by Soongsil University Press
156-743, 369 Sangdo-Ro, Dongjak-Gu, Seoul, Kore
http://press.ssu.ac.kr
Tel: 02-820-0771~2
ISBN 978-89-7450-291-1

The world of sounds is full of interesting stories and great tales. Sounds are around us everywhere we go, and we humans communicate with each other using speech sounds. Whether or not you are aware of it, sounds are always around you, making you relaxed, delighted, focused, annoyed, nervous, distracted, or even terrified. TV commercials, movie producers, and popular song makers add special sound effects to better market their products. Indeed, sounds are an effective and powerful tool in meeting various needs.

This book is about the sounds we hear in everyday life. The following chapters include stories about sounds of human speech; the natural sounds of animals and sounds of animals imitating human speech; sounds of insects; sounds of musical instruments; sounds of natural surroundings like wind, waterfalls, birds, pebbles, and waves. There is also a cautionary tale about noise-deafness as a result of wearing earphones for too long or listening to music with earphones at too high a volume.

Some stories are based on scientific reasons and evidences, while others are exciting undiscovered secrets about sounds. We are sure that you will be surprised to see how many great stories of sounds can be found around you.

As colleagues at Soongsil University, we have worked together to write this book. Professor Bae, Myungjin (Ph.D. in Engineering, School of Electronic Engineering, Soongsil University, and the head of the Sound Engineering Research Institute at Soongsil University) is the most well-known scholar and researcher in sound engineering in Korea. He has become a recognized and trusted scholar in the field through numerous academic achievements as well as countless appearances on TV programs. For this book, he wrote essays explaining sounds from a scientific point of view. Since he is interested in a variety of subjects on sound, anything related to sound may be a topic of future research for him. Professor Kim, Myungsook (Ph.D. in English, Dept. of English Language and Literature, Soongsil University, and a participating researcher of the Sound Engineering Research Institute at Soongsil University) is a linguist specializing in the sound systems of the English Language. She is interested not only in human speech sounds, but also socio-linguistic aspects of sounds like differences in voice tone between men and women. For this book, she wrote essays explaining human speech sounds, and related stories, from a linguistic point of view.

We hope that this book will inspire not only college students majoring in relevant fields but also the general public. We also hope that the book provides each and every reader with basic knowledge of how to work with sounds for their own purposes.

Special thanks go out to the publishing office of Soongsil University for kindly accepting our proposal to publish this book. Professor Michelle Andrus (Dept. of English Language and Literature, Soongsil University) has done a great job in proofreading final drafts of the book. The most notable contributor to this book is SOUND.

Welcome to the world of sound! We hope you enjoy reading these great tales of sound.

September 2012

Bae, Myungjin and Kim, Myungsook

Contents

We usually get the urge to laugh when someone next to us is laughing uproariously. Sound waves for laughter have a viral effect in that they make other people laugh as well. In addition, every laughter has its own phonation that reminds people of funny moments in their lifetime. When you begin to laugh, your vocal cords vibrate and tickle themselves and your vocal bands stretch, perpetuating laughter that is hard to stop.

When one person smiles, another smile as well. Why don't you smile along with me?

I recently did a consultation that involved 'laughing dogs.' My client asked me to record the sounds of a laughing dog and have them played to different dogs, and see if they would laugh along or not, in the agreeable setting of an animal farm. It was quite an interesting suggestion.

Dog lovers know that dogs make unique sounds when people play with them. With this in mind, we invited from across the country families who believe their dogs laughed when they played, in order to record the sound of laughing dogs. At first, dogs seemed to act normally, with their tongues hanging out as they breathed in short breaths. Then, the dogs seemed to be frowning as they played with their owners, but I realized that the sounds they were making were quite different from the sounds that the dogs would make under normal conditions.

When we analyzed the sound spectrum of those sounds, it turned out that the sounds created by dog's laughter contained a different spectrum from that of usual dog sounds. In order to compare the difference more accurately, two more sounds were recorded from the laughing dogs: the first while they were resting and the second after a short running session. We found that the frequency range was between 1,000-2,000 Hz after they ran, indicating a mid-range tone. But when they laughed, the frequency was at a higher state of over 2,000 Hz, even when they were resting. This means that when dogs laugh, their breathing shortens and the tempo of the laughter increases, creating a brief but repetitive "heu, heu, heu-heu" sound at a high frequency.

However, dogs don't have a variety of kinds of laughter. This is due to their anatomical structure wherein the sound is created as air tickles the throat, not resonates as in human breath. This is why dogs can't create resonant sounds, while people can produce different types of sounds by using resonance in the vocal tract. Thus, dogs can only make a 'heu-heu' sound, but their pulse will increase and their breaths shorten due to heightened emotion. Most people cannot distinguish whether their dogs are laughing or just breathing fast.

Next, we recorded one dog's laughter and played it to

Laughing dogs-Most people cannot distinguish whether their dogs are laughing or just breathing fast

another dog after deleting all residual noises alongside the laughter. The second dog began to react to the 'laughter,' changing its facial expression and creating a repetitive sound at a short tempo. The laughing virus spread among the dogs and created a rather lively atmosphere in the farm. Dogs of many species were 'laughing' together along with this recorded dog 'laughter' coming out of a machine.

Human laughter can be categorized roughly into three groups: 'Kek-kek-kek,' like that of Yu, Jae-suk, a popular Korean comedian; 'oo-ha ha ha,' like that of Kang, Ho-dong, a pre-professional wrestler and TV entertainer in Korea; or 'ha-a-a-a,' like that of Lee, Kyung-shil, a female Korean show host. I laughed as well while analyzing the sounds of different laughter. I believe the laughing virus infected me, too. 'Oo-ha, ha-ha!' Why don't you laugh along with me?

Three representative groups of people's laughter: the group of You, Jae-suk, the group of Kang, Ho-dong, and the group of Lee, Kyung-shil.

With the staff members of the SBS program, *Animal Farms*

Parents usually get nervous when children suddenly cry out and whine. This is because they may not understand the hidden meaning behind children's crying. Most children are believed to cry for a reason. If they do, what kind of meaning is hidden in each type of crying? We tried to compare the sounds of Korean children's crying to those of children from other countries.

First, we recorded babies' cry in the hospital and separated the cries into several different categories with the help of experienced nurses, as previously done in a foreign case study. Then, the recordings were uploaded to a website, and mothers who had recently given birth were asked to carefully listen to the babies' cries and identify them into different categories with respect to sound and situation.

We were able to come up with 5 different categories. The first type of crying occurs when babies are physically sick. It sounds like 'eu-ah, eu-ah' with a bit of weeping towards the end. In a short period of time, the change of tone (low-high-low) is preceded by a low but long weeping sound that lasts for longer than 0.5 seconds. It is a sound to alert mothers to the pain babies are having. Babies who cry this way are usually frowning and cry from time to time. They may even have a fever as well.

The second type of crying occurs when babies are annoyed by something. The cry may sound like 'ah-oong, ah-oong.' The first syllable is accentuated whereas the 'oong' part softly dissipates. It is possible to hear a compressed sound made by the throat (for about 0.5 seconds) in the middle of vocalizing the 'ah-oong' sound. It is rare

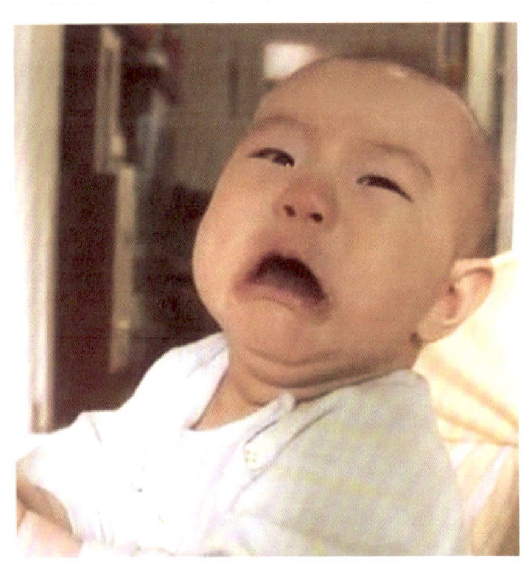

Babeis cry for a reason

to see tears with this type of crying. Babies will usually stop crying when their environment is adjusted, for example, with a change of diapers, or when they are moved to a quiet location.

The third type of crying occurs when babies are under great stress. People might think babies don't feel any pressure or anxiety, but they are prone to stress as well. Babies produce the sound 'eu-ah-ahng, eu-ah-ahng' for longer than a second per cry with an annoyed tone. This type of crying can be heard when babies feel too cold or too hot due to wet diapers or when they are in an uncomfortable position. The difference between the second type and the third type of crying is that the latter has a prolonged sound, especially when babies compress their throat as they cry. They often cry with this sound when something is urgently needed, and the crying is usually accompanied by kicking and tears.

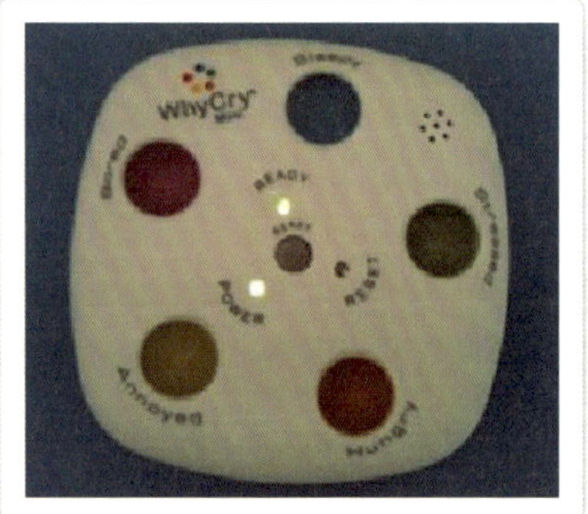

Baby-cry translators are available on the market (The image captured from an ad for a baby-cry translator)

The fourth type of crying occurs when babies are sleepy. Usually this type of crying doesn't have any strength in it. We usually call it a whimpering noise, where there is either multiple repetitions of 'eu' or a short but continuous 'eu-ahng,' or a short staccato 'eu' that lasts less than 1 second. You might have seen children whimper and fall asleep as these sounds soften and eventually disappear.

The last type of crying occurs when babies are hungry. This is the strongest and most aggressive sound among all five types. Babies take hunger seriously. In order to satisfy their need, they will cry 'eung-ae, eung-ae' until their need is met. The 'eung' sound tends to be short, followed by a longer 'ae.' The tone is relatively maintained at a stable level for over 1 second. This sound is very different from the other sounds.

All these types of crying were basically similar to those examined in the foreign case study. In conclusion, babies' types of crying have the same basic characteristics across the globe across all races and ethnicities. It is imperative to understand that babies are born with the innate ability to make sounds, or cries, that substitute for spoken language for them to communicate with others. It is this language that must be understood by parents.

3

A Boy Who Can See with Sound

A producer from the TV program *Instant Capture: How Could This Be* called me one day. He told me there was a blind child in the United States who could ride a bike and inline skate only by making sounds with his mouth. He wanted to know if it was possible to analyze this phenomenon and have an interview with me about the result. I was surprised. It meant that there was a person who could 'see' his surroundings using a high-pitched frequency without actually looking at them with his eyes, just like a bat that utilizes an ultra-pitched sound for hunting in darkness.

We usually knock on a bathroom door to see if it is oc-

Bats fly in the darkness with ultra-sonic sensing ability

cupied. The knocking makes sound waves in the air, and we wait for a response as a result of that knocking. This child uses a similar method, but he uses his tongue to 'knock' on the air, and the sound waves produced by this reverberating 'knock' travel back to his ears and allow him to 'see' objects around him. He produces a 'tahk-tahk' sound that covers a wide sound range: his tongue touches the palatal area of the mouth and makes this tapping sound. When this noise with a wide sound range hits an object, the frequency at which the object reflects is bounced back, creating different waves of resonance. The boy is able to distinguish the shape of an object with these waves of resonance.

Human ears can distinguish the location of objects by

hearing a sound bounce off them. When sound travels through a standard medium, it moves at a speed of 340 m/sec until it hits an object. Assuming that two objects are 2 meters apart, the actual sound and its eco will have a time difference of less than 1/100 second. The child is able to compute the surrounding objects' locations within this time frame! That is, he figures out the different heights of objects and their relative locations in a very short time and freely moves around only with a couple of 'tahk-tahk' noises.

He travels long distances without the aid of his service dog, dodges around moving vehicles on the street, and even plays video games with his friends and wins just by hearing sound from the speakers. How did the boy come to possess this ability? According to the boy, his mother trained his sense of direction through listening. When he was born

Today, cars are equipped with rear sensor systems

blind, an attempt was made to give him vision, but it failed. The child followed his mother everywhere she went. She would walk around the house, and play hide and seek while making 'tahk-tahk' sounds so that the child could follow them and find her.

When cars are in reverse, parking-aid sensors create a high-frequency sound, where the repetition of a 'pih-pih-pih' sound increases as the car moves closer to an object. When people are blind, they must rely on their other four senses without the aid of vision. As we have seen in the boy's case, it shouldn't be a big problem to live a relatively normal life if one can master the technique used by the boy, who makes full use of the sound created by his tongue to distinguish objects around him.

Humans can identify the location as well as the height of objects around them by recognizing a minute difference in frequencies in projected sounds heard by their ears. This phenomenon is called the binaural beat. Modern technology utilizes this beat to improve the power of concentration and learning abilities by stimulating brain waves with the sounds in accordance with the hearing characteristics of each person. Recently, the binaural beat has also been used to induce deep sleep for people suffering from insomnia.

Meanwhile, the sounds projected by so-called cyber drug boost the binaural beat to induce brain waves that are ag-

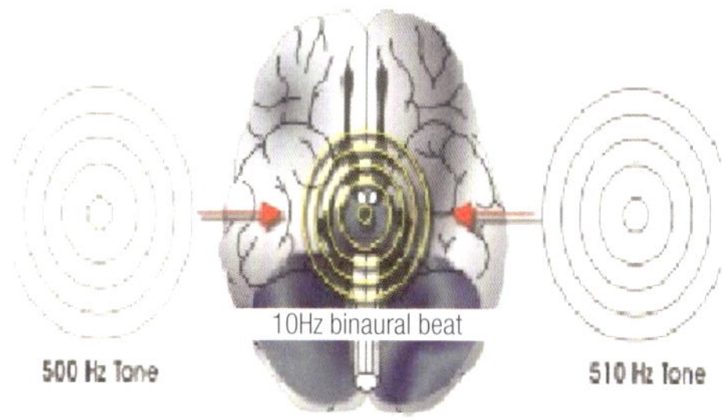

The binaural beat negatively stimulates the brain waves by controlling the differences in hearing through each ear

gressive and convoluted. Cyber drugs use the theory of negatively stimulating brain waves by controlling the difference in hearing through each ear and thus result in hallucinations achieved solely through sound. To maximize the effects of cyber drugs, it is advised to use headsets instead of speakers or earphones so that the sounds can directly reach our eardrums.

Certain problems arise when we listen to these sounds.

Cyber drugs eventually disable our hearing and dull our minds (The image captured from an ad for a cyber drug)

Listening to a cyber drug even one time should be avoided (The image illustrated by *Kookmin Ilbo*)

First and foremost, there is a problem with the intensity of the amplitude, or the volume of the sounds. To maximize the effects of the cyber drug, high volume is required; however, listening to loud noise for over 30 minutes can result in noise deafness.

The pitch of such a sound can be a problem as well. The cyber drug is made up of 100 Hz to 300 Hz sounds, which are known as pure sound. Listening to such sounds for about 5 minutes can cause someone to feel dazed and gradually become dull-minded, and can cause the body to feel lazy and eventually stressed out. Furthermore, the vast gap in sound frequencies and amplitudes between the two ears has the equivalent effect of a siren, and can cause mood changes. Continually hearing such sound for 10 minutes can lead us to feel angry and violent. Even after we stop listening to a cyber drug, the sounds may continue in the mind and alter our behavioral patterns. As time goes by, a cyber drug may cause damage to a person's brain, and thus cause a person to be unstable.

The effects of a cyber drug may vary from person to person. For example, those with good mental health are not easily affected by the sounds and only hear some noise. However, those with low self-esteem are easily affected by the sounds.

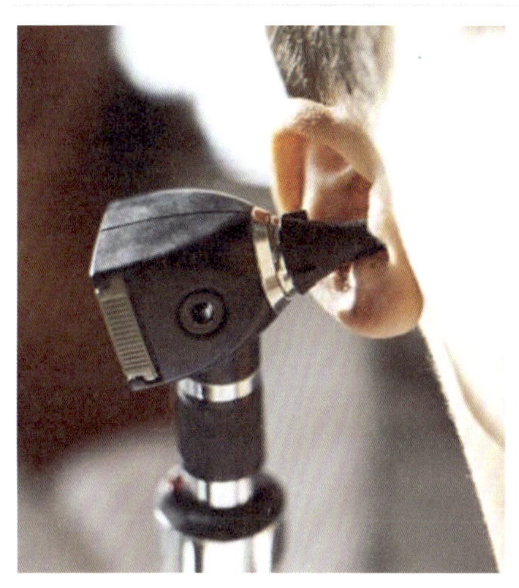

Cyber drugs may cause noise-induced hearing loss

The sounds of a cyber drug travel through the ears directly to our brain. The simple yet repetitive sound specifically stimulates our auditory cells and brain, leaving a trace that eventually leads to addiction. Moreover, children and teenagers who are not mature enough to protect themselves are easily susceptible to cyber drugs, and so we should be more cautious about the use of cyber drugs.

Since cyber drugs can make society lethargic and/or violent, we should not be hasty about setting up a judicial punishment system. A more careful approach to maintaining the general order of society should be considered as a first solution to this kind of drug. People must be alerted and its sources for downloading must be shut down at the very beginning stage. Listening to a cyber drug even one time purely out of curiosity should be avoided. We must alert people to stay away from cyber drugs, because they are harmful to our mental health.

5 Tasty Sounds

Chilly spring weather with light rain showers creates a melancholic mood for many. Most people say spring rain soothes their mind and soul, but for me it reminds me of my childhood: When it rained, I used to eat Korean pizza (*boo-chim-gae*) cooked by my mother.

One day not too long ago, a broadcasting company called me for my expertise, asking me to test an old Korean saying: "When it rains, I want to eat *boo-chim-gae*." Of course, this doesn't strictly mean a specific type of *boo-chim-gae*, but any type of Korean pizza (with kimchi or with green onions or with whatever ingredients). The question is, why do people

In spring, we hear the cheerful pitter-patter of raindrops, which causes in people an urge to eat *boo-chim-gae* and/or *Kal-gook-soo*

eat *boo-chim-gae* when it rains?

After recording rain, I realized there are many different types of sounds to it: the sound of heavy rain during the monsoon season, the sound of strong and noisy rain striking a roof made up of metal sheets, the sound of intermittently sprinkling rain, of light rain, of gloomy winter rain, and of many more kinds of rain. Each season also has its own sounds of rain with distinct characteristics. So the question is, 'What type of rain sound causes in people an urge to eat *boo-chim-gae*?'

It was not the winter rain, the monsoon rain, or the gloomy autumn rain. From our survey conducted with the support of sound analysis, it was concluded that people have an urge to eat *boo-chim-gae* when they hear the sound of rain during the spring season. It was the sound of water droplets falling from the edge of the roof, the sound of rain hitting the window, and the sound of sprinkling showers mixed with the light breeze of spring wind. We recorded all the sounds from spring rain and analyzed them in comparison with the sound of *boo-chim-gae* being made. We also recorded the sound of oil sizzling while a Korean pizza is being made. Then, a comparison was made between the sound when water meets oil and the sound of spring rain hitting a window.

Surprisingly, these two sounds, which may be considered very different from one another, turned out to have similar amplitudes and frequencies. The sound of batter entering an oiled pan may sound different than the sound of rain and wind mixed together, but the qualities of the two sounds are very similar in their amplitudes and frequencies. Some sound engineers even had difficulty distinguishing between the two sounds when they analyzed them. They are basically the same sounds.

The use of sound effects is easily observed in media, especially in commercials related to food. The slurping sound of eating noodles, or the fizzing sound of carbonated drinks, or the sound of a beer cap explosion followed by the sizzling sound of pouring beer--all these sounds are used to stimulate our sense of hunger. They may also be used as a mechanism to remember when we ate a certain kind of food.

People say that restaurants or take-out shops for *kal-gook-soo*(a kind of Korean noodle) or assorted fried foods including *boo-chim-gae* have good sales on rainy days. Not surprisingly, the sound of soup boiling while *kal-gook-soo* is made resembles that of *boo-chim-gae* being made and, concurrently, that of spring rain. Sounds stimulate brain activity, leading us to think of certain items that are closely related to the sounds we are hearing. The relationship between a sound and the image created can be used effectively in successful marketing strategies to increase sales and perhaps better our health. In other cultures, we may similarly find interesting associations between different rain sounds and different foods.

The sizzling sounds of a Korean pizza are a good match for the sound of raindrops

6

Healthy Hearing, Healthy Society

We may face uncomfortable moments on the subway when the person sitting next to us has their earphone volume turned up to maximum. Changing seats gets rid of our discomfort. However, the actual problem really belongs to that person, not us. Listening to loud noise can create 'noise induced deafness.' Noise induced deafness means your hearing becomes impaired due to continual exposure to loud noise, and your hearing 'age' increases at a faster rate.

Young adults should be able to hear high-frequency sounds and small noises, but nowadays many of them are not able to hear these sounds anymore. An experiment done at a college indicates that more than 30% of college students in their 20s are not able to hear a 15,000 Hz sound, a sound that should be easily heard until one's mid 30s, on average. What is causing this trend? One of the main reasons is the prolonged use of headsets or earphones. These devices continuously stimulate the sensory cells of the ears, and when worn for long periods of time, lead to deafness to high-frequency sounds, and ultimately, to deafness to all sounds.

On average, college students set their volume at 80% capacity and listen to music for about an hour. When they do so, the sound traveling through the ear is at approximately 85 dB. This level increases to 96 dB when it comes to delivery men who listen to music while riding their motorcycles. 95 dB is equivalent to measurement an average of the sound of

We can find many people wearing earphones in public places

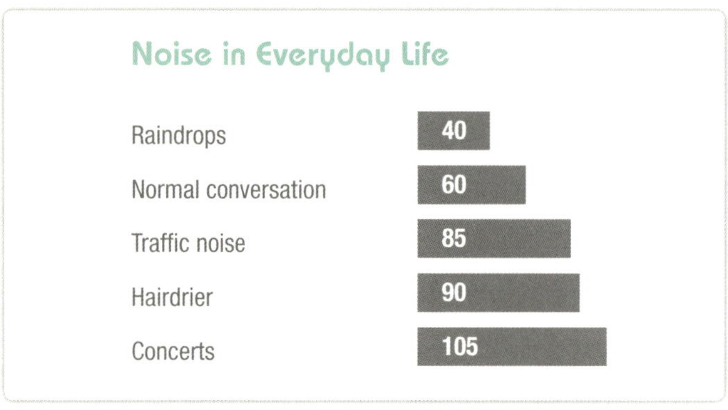

Amplitudes of different noises in everyday life (unit : dB)

thunder and the reverberations in a karaoke room(or a singing room). It is amazing that our tympanic membrane can take such a beating.

Improving your hearing is generally quite difficult. Moreover, once the tympanic membrane is damaged, it is nearly impossible to reverse the condition. Reduced range of sound can create many difficulties. In serious cases, people in their 50s may need to use a hearing aid, that is usually for people in their 70s. Inevitably, people can't help but further increase the volume of what they are listening to, and this will worsen their condition, leading to deafness to all sounds.

People may think being unable to hear small noises isn't that critical in our lives, but its repercussions are serious. Korean language is syllable-timed, and each syllable consists of onset (initial consonant), nucleus (vowel), and coda (final consonant, but this is an optional element for a syllable in Korean). Initial and final consonants are usually heard at 2,500 Hz or higher. Therefore, people with noise induced deafness may not be able to speak correctly because they can't hear the differences between the two, the initial and final consonants, so their voices get louder as a result, creating a 'loud' society.

Furthermore, if people can hear only low-frequency sounds, the organ of corti cannot detect high-frequency noises and may create an overall feeling of discomfort. This can lead to depression and detachment for individuals and could eventually create a melancholic society.

Going back to the subway situation, the sound we hear from someone else's earphones may annoy us. Earphones are usually designed to have small holes on the outside for the sound to travel at maximum capacity for the listener. Some sounds leak from these holes and travel at 3,000-4,000 Hz. The human ear can easily hear sounds at this frequency range, and the earphones create pure tone which can cause annoyance and discomfort to people sitting nearby.

Fortunately, noise induced deafness can be prevented with some attention and care in its early stages. If possible, avoid prolonged exposure to earphones and use speakers instead. Regular speakers produce a wide range of sounds with background noises heard in everyday life, positively reducing the pressures on your ears. If you must use earphones, listen to music at a lower level, at 50-60% of maximum volume.

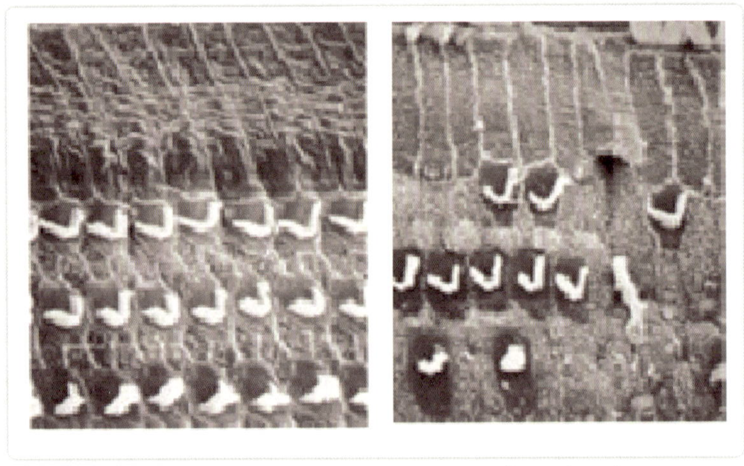

Normal ear cells

Damaged ear cells

Damage to ear cells occurs as noise-induced hearing loss develops

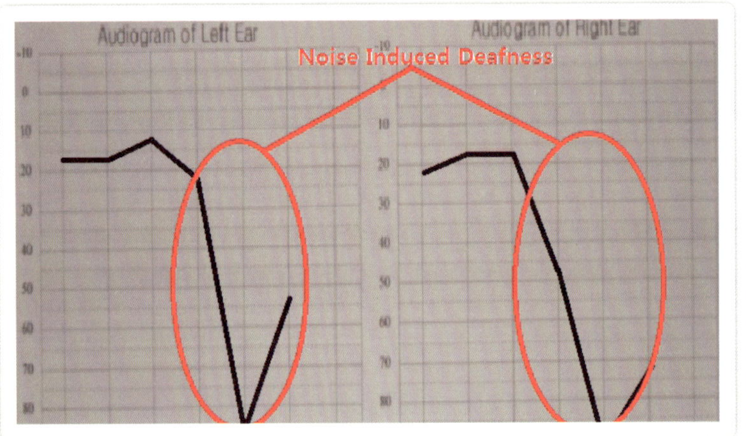

High-frequency sounds are hard to hear when you suffer from noise-induced hearing loss

7

Lee, Mi-Ja's Voice, Naturally Wonderful

There are many cultures in the world in which singing and/or listening to music are very common and popular, and young adults today in many countries go "everywhere" with earphones in and music playing. Most young adults usually wear their earphones to listen to music, and karaoke rooms have become part of the mainstream entertainment. Among the five human senses of smelling, seeing, touching, tasting, and hearing, the auditory sense, hearing, is the most easily satiable in this culture.

Therefore, using sound in the current market system adds value to the products more effectively. This can be seen in the

Lee, Mi-ja has been a popular singer in Korea for more than 40 years

most watched TV programs for auditioning new singers, as well as in various kinds of competition programs for singers, hence raising popularity and market value for singers with their music. So, we may raise a question, "Does this mean popular singers create sounds that are different from those made by regular people?" I have been asked by a broadcasting company to analyze the voice of 72-year-old female singer Lee, Mi-Ja, one of the most popular singers in Korea.

According to Samsung's Economy Research team, Lee, Mi-Ja's songs have a value of 165 billions Korean won. This value includes concert revenues and is indicative of her influence in the market. Her 46-year career of singing has given us approximately 560 albums and 2,069 songs. Album sales number are somewhere in the 15 million to 20 million range.

Lee, Mi-Ja once said in an interview, "I couldn't even visit an orthodontist to get treatment for my teeth irregularities because I was afraid my voice would change." She was right, as the shape of the inside space of her mouth would have changed, resulting in a different voice, if she had been treat-

Most professional singers have big mouths and long necks

ed by an orthodontist.

There is a popular belief that people with big mouths can sing better. Lee, Mi-Ja has quite a big mouth compared to that of other people. This means she has more space inside her mouth, which can create bigger echoes and thus bigger sounds. But having a big mouth doesn't necessarily mean one will be a better singer. Vocal chords and voice production play an important role in singing as well.

In the analysis of a couple of her early works, such as *Teacher from an Island* and *Lady Camellia*, I found an interesting point. Her voice production range is exceptionally wide with a high degree of vocal chord vibration.

According to our voice-analyzing instrument, her tone was very clear with harmonics that rivaled musical instruments. Even at a higher-frequency range, where it is difficult to sustain stable vibrato, her voice was very stable. She was able to move up and down 3 octaves with ease and stability. I believe that it is her ability to create vibrato in any range covering low, middle, and high-frequencies that produces a feeling of sorrow in listeners.

What is more surprising is that her voice in her 20s and that in her 60s do not show much change. It is usual to see a change in timbre with a narrowing of the sound range as people get older, but this has not been so in Lee, Mi-Ja's case.

It can be concluded that she was born with a gift of finely developed vocal bands. The Creator has given her the best instrument of sound that any human could have.

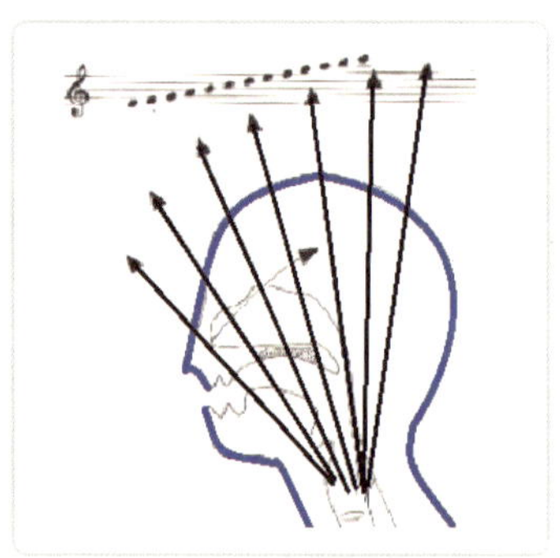

An imaginary picture showing that Lee, Mi-Ja is able to move her voice up and down 3 octaves with ease and stability

8 Hand Bells Draw Our Attention!

Around the Christmas season, we very often hear the sounds of hand bells from the Salvation Army. In the midst of traffic noise and the indistinguishable sounds of crowds, the crisp sound of bells can be easily heard from all directions. We sometimes look into our wallets to see if we can help the poor and find ourselves walking towards the red basket. This behavior is promoted by the sound itself. Our brain processes the bell's rhythm, 'Ttaeng-geu-rung,' which calls to us.

In fact, we hear many sounds when the bell is struck. First, we hear the harmonic sound of 'Chaeng-chaeng', consisting of a wide frequency range of 6 kHz-20 kHz. Then

The crisp sound of hand bells can be easily heard from afar and in all directions

there comes the pure tone of 'ttaeng' at 3 kHz-4 kHz, followed by the harmonic sound of 'geu-rung.'

Although our hearing can theoretically detect anywhere between 20 Hz-20 kHz of sound, we don't hear every sound within this range with the same degree of perception. If the sound range deviates below or above 3.5 kHz, the base line of the audible range, it gets harder for us to detect sound. If we want to make a 100 Hz drum producing a sound of 3.5 kHz, the sound pressure must be increased by 35 dB for easy hearing.

The first harmonic sound covering 6 kHz-20 kHz is not a sound range people hear in everyday life activities. According to the research, when we hear a sound within this range, our auditory receptors are stimulated at a wide sound range that creates the feeling of calmness and satisfaction.

On the other hand, the basic pure tone created by a hand

bell covering the range of 3 kHz-4 kHz can be detected by people quite well. As mentioned before, we can detect the sound within this range quite clearly and easily even with background noise.

The design of a hand bell contributes to its characteristic sounds and tempo

If hand bells were designed to produce sounds only between 3 kHz-4 kHz, it would probably irritate us like the /ppi-/ sound of bus cards swiped to get on and off buses. However, when the clapper strikes the ring of the hand bell, it creates another basic pure tone of high frequency covering 5 kHz-6 kHz together with a background overtone within the range of 6 kHz-20 kHz, resulting in harmony and chords among the sounds. The mixture of overtones and high frequency sounds create something that is quite pleasing to hear.

The design of a hand bell also contributes to its characteristic sounds and tempo (approximately 1 strike per 1.5 sec), which remind us of the images of the Salvation Army and poor people. The weight and volume of the bell prevents people from striking the bell at a faster rate. We are thus able to hear a hand bell from afar, where its pure tone is pleasing to hear with its lively harmonics and 1.5-second interval of tempo, which relax us.

We may find the positive use of high frequency sounds all around us. For example, we often hear high frequency sounds in everyday life, such as Korean candy sellers of a county fair strike broken scissors together. Striking scissors produce a group of sounds within the range of 6 kHz-8 kHz that stimulates our brain and calls for our attention. When we see the candy seller and hear these sounds, our curiosity locks on to them and the candies as well.

In some countries, high frequency sounds are used to treat people who are suffering from depression or mental challenges. These rare sounds are refreshing light on the ears and lively

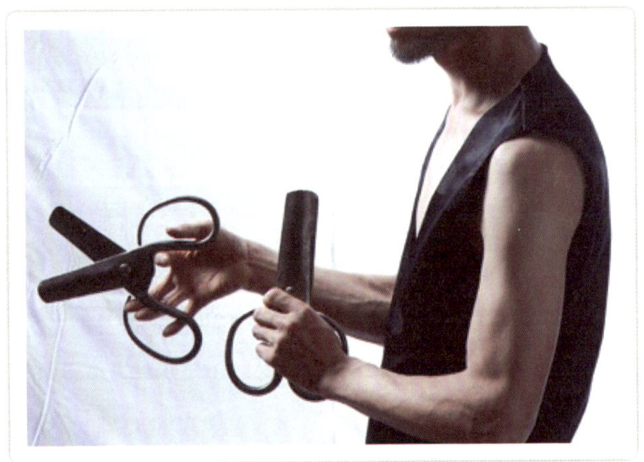

We often hear high-frequency sounds in everyday life, such as when Korean candy sellers at a county fair strike broken scissors together

enough to draw people out of depression. For mentally challenged people, the sounds stimulate latent auditory sense so that the people can feel active and energetic.

In the middle of a loud crowd, we are very much attracted to the sound of the hand bell with its high frequency, as well as its overtone, and are likely to put money into the basket. When the bell is struck, the sound of pure tones travels easily and clearly to our brain, providing pleasing harmonics and comfort.

9

The Spirit of South Africa World Cup: The Sound of the Vuvuzela

In June of 2010, the people of Korea had long been awaiting the World Cup with hopes of making the semi-final round once again as in 2002. Korea had a game against one of the leading contenders, Argentina. Banners and posters could be seen on every street throughout the cities of Korea, and we could feel the excitement of the soccer field through our televisions and radios.

Even before the game started, as soon as the live broadcasting began and we could see the soccer field on the TV screen, the sound of cheering 'Wah' erupted. In the midst of the mix of many sounds and noises, we often heard the

The vuvuzela is a simple-looking South African traditional wind instrument that extends 50-150 cm

'Ttae-ttae' sound of vuvuzelas. The vuvuzela is a simple-looking South African traditional wind instrument that extends 50-150 cm.

The vuvuzela makes a fundamental tone through the mouth piece (20-25 Hz) due to the absence of holes on the body, creating a resonance with simple sounds. The length of the instrument decides the resonance characteristics, producing over 20 different harmonics that can reach the high end of 2,500 Hz. People are usually disturbed by the sound of the vuvuzela because it is produced at a constant pitch without much oscillation. Furthermore, people are usually very sensitive to this sound range.

The vuvuzela is also a very loud instrument. It creates a stunning 130 dB of sound at the opening of the instrument, which rivals the sound of a jet engine on take off. If people are exposed to sounds at this volume for over 30 minutes, they will very likely suffer from having noise induced deafness. Therefore, it is advisable for spectators to wear earplugs or noise cancellation headsets, although these aids won't block the noise completely and some people may suffer.

The vuvuzela contains a very wide range of sound and amplitude that can easily irritate the human ear. What makes matters worse is that it doesn't have a unifying rhythm nor any consistent frequency. The sound depends solely on the breathing capacity and intensity of the person playing it. Playing the vuvuzela may relieve stress for the person playing it, but the sound doesn't encourage any unified spirit among people in cheering. Having no rhythm and tempo, the sound of the vuvuzela annoys other audience members,

During the World Cup in South Africa, vuvuzelas were everywhere among the spectators

the way hyenas gathering for a meal would, causing listeners to become emotionally unstable.

Kim, Heung-Kook, a famous Korean comedian and soccer mania, who attended the game, said that he couldn't see or hear the sound of the *kkwaenggwari* or traditional Korean drums in the stadium. While the vuvuzela produce 130 dB of sound, *kkwaenggwari* produces only 115 dB. The 'kwa-gang' sound of the *kweng-ga-ri* lasts about 0.2 seconds and dissipates, but the sound of vuvuzelas depends on the person's breathing capacity, and can last for quite a few seconds.

What kind of effect does the vuvuzela have on the players on the field? At first, they feel annoyance similar to that of the audience. Sounds of multiple vuvuzelas from afar merge together to create something called white noise, which resembles the sound of a large group of bees buzzing: 'ttae, ttae.' In the sound spectrum, the resonance and frequency of the vuvuzela match those of bees buzzing at 1,000 Hz. Athletes may confuse the collective sound of the instruments for a group of bees buzzing nearby.

Fortunately, the sound of the vuvuzela can be comforting to players if they are exposed to the sound for a long time. As the sound becomes background noise, the players are able to get used to it. They may even think fans are cheering for their team, and thus they may play harder. However, as far as the attending audience or television audience are concerned, the noise is more likely to sound like a racket, and they probably wish to escape it.

Our research team has tried to reduce the sound of vuvuzelas in various ways, and we came up with the idea of reducing the sound range of the instrument, which covers 250 Hz all the way to 2,500 Hz, by adjusting the equalizer. YTN, the news broadcasting company, and the *Chosun Daily Newspaper*, each took our advice and reported about the way to adjust the equalizer of TV sets at home, in order to reduce the noise of the instrument and increase the volume of the commentary.

However, there is an even better way of reducing the sound of the vuvuzela heard on television. There is technology developed to track certain noises on television and reduce them in real time. We provided this tip as technical advisor to SBS Broadcasting Company, the company in charge of broadcasting the World Cup Games to Korea. BBC also had similar technology and said they would be implement-

The resonance and frequency of the vuvuzela match those of bees buzzing at 1,000 Hz

ing it on television for their broadcasting of the World Cup Games. Tracking the noise in real time and reducing unwanted noise while preserving wanted sounds such as that of commentaries creates a better sound transfer on TV.

Let's return to the sound of the *kkwaenggwari*. People from other countries could not recognize the sounds of the *kkwaenggwari* and other traditional Korean drums at the 2002 World Cup Games because they were new to them. The famous cheer of '*Dae-han-min-kook*' in a unique rhythmic pattern was also not understood at first. A similar situation took place in South Africa because of the vuvuzela and its noisy sound. Although it would be nearly impossible to ban the instrument from this worldwide event, we can use our advanced technology to reduce the unwanted sound before it gets to TV audiences, and meanwhile keep on hoping that the Korean soccer team will make it to the semifinals again in the future.

BBC consider 'vuvuzela free' World Cup audio

By Sherna Noah, Press Association

Tuesday, 15 June 2010

SHARE PRINT EMAIL A A TEXT SIZE

The BBC is considering whether to broadcast a "vuvuzela free" version of its World Cup coverage following complaints about the noise from the plastic horn.

The Corporation is investigating several options, including stripping out most sound except commentary when showing the games on its red button digital service.

Related articles

- Could the vuvuzela become the sound of British football?
- Vuvuleza: There's no excuse for making a din when you've been taught by the experts

Search the news archive for more stories

CARL DE SOUZA/AFP/GETTY IMAGES

A football fan blows an extra-long vuvuzela horn on the first day of the 2010 World Cup in Cape Town

ENLARGE

Complaints about the incessant buzzing noise doubled to 545 to the BBC by this morning.

A BBC spokeswoman said: "Using the red button service is only one of the options that we're considering. A decision will be

BBC broadcasted the World Cup games after removing the sound of vuvuzelas (from BBC homepage http://www.bbc.co.uk)

10 An Elephant Can Speak Korean!

Smart dogs, cats, and other animals can understand what we say to them, but it is very difficult for them to mimic our voice. The differences in the structure of their oral cavity, the shape of their vocal tract, and their level of intelligence prevent them from mimicking human language. But some exceptions are seen from time to time. A couple of years ago, I got a phone call from a zookeeper at Everland, an amusement park in Korea. He told me that one of the elephants in the zoo seemed to be saying some Korean words and wanted my expertise.

This would be one of the most surprising and exciting

Koshik, the talking elephant, is talking to its breeder

cases if the elephant truly produced human speech words. Elephants' speech organs are not as developed as those of humans. They usually make 'bhoo' noises when they are scared, but for the most part, they stay calm and quiet, making no audible sound. However, they actually do create sounds at very low frequency (lower than 20 Hz), which humans can't hear, and they communicate with each other making sounds within this range.

When I played the video clip sent by the zookeeper, I couldn't believe what I heard and saw. An elephant named *Koshik* was saying Korean words like 'nu-woh' (lie down), 'il-eo-nah' (stand up) and 'an-jjah' (let's sit). *Koshik* also said 'jo-ah' (I like it), 'dol-ah' (turn around), 'ahn-doe' (no), 'bahl' (foot), and simple sentences like 'uhl-jjahng-it-nae' (Here the good looking one is.). The pronunciation wasn't perfect, but I was able to understand the words.

When we obserbed *Koshik* saying these words and sentences, we found that when we tried to mimic the zookeeper's voice, he would insert his trunk into his mouth. As if shaping the mouth to whistle, *Koshik* varied the depth of the insertion and twisted his trunk in his mouth to change the airway to produce human speech sounds. He seemed to be trying to make various shapes in the airway by dilating and constricting the nose to create different sounds. This resembles the way which humans articulate different sounds, for example changing sounds from ‘hoo’ to ‘ch-ch,’ by closing their mouth to release the sound through their teeth.

In the acoustic analysis of the two sounds, one produced by *Koshik* and the other by the zookeeper, we found that the two sounds were very similar in many respects. First, the frequencies of the basic tone in the two sounds were approximately the same at 130 Hz for *Koshik* and 132 Hz for the zookeeper. The resonance range was also very similar between the two, with *Koshik*'s at 570-2,650 Hz and the zookeeper's at 550-2,400 Hz. It is safe to conclude that both were producing similar sounds. What's more surprising is that the zookeeper's and *Koshik*'s vocal characteristics measuring as 94% similar. When two sounds resemble each other more than 90%, it is very difficult to distinguish differences between them.

Koshik not only obeyed the commands of the zookeeper by understanding his words, but tried to articulate the sounds, which were beyond his own vocal capacity. It is certain that the elephant wanted to communicate with humans, the zookeeper in particular. I have read about an elephant in Germany that mimics the sound of a truck's engine-'D-rung, D-rung'-which caused a big sensation when introduced in an article in Nature. Now, I'm proud to say that, for the first time in the history, there is an elephant that has succeeded in producing human speech sounds, the Korean language in particular, and is able to communicate with people.

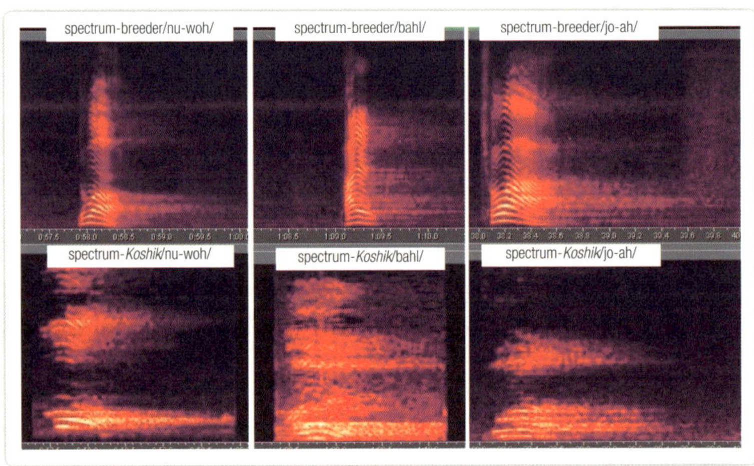

The spectrums of *Koshik*'s pronunciation compared to those of the breeder's pronunciation

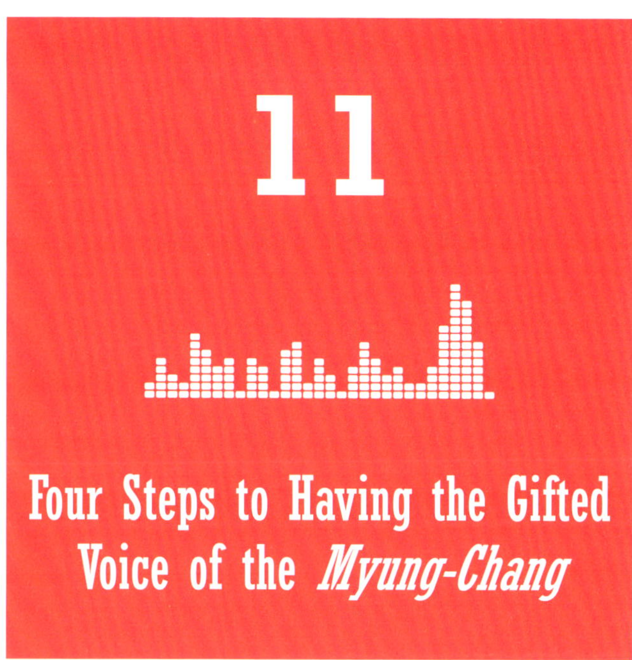

11 Four Steps to Having the Gifted Voice of the *Myung-Chang*

A *myung-chang* is someone who has been accredited by the government as a master singer of *Pansori* or *Minyo*, kind of traditional Korean songs. To become a *myung-chang*, one must reach a level some people define by saying 'You must practice hard enough to have spit blood three times.' To be honest, I think a person can become a good singer if he or she has a beautiful voice along with an artistic sense of tempo and tune. So, why do people say 'you must spit blood three times'?

Traditional training places to develop the gifted voice of a *myung-chang*

In 2003, *Pansori* was proclaimed Intangible Cultural Heritage of Humanity by UNESCO in the category of opera. In order to perform a work of *Pansori*, a singer should sing and speak continuously for three or four hours per session in a loud and clear voice. This requires a tremendous amount of energy and a myriad of voice characteristics. It should be interesting to find out what necessary steps it is believed people should follow if they want to learn the art of *Pansori*.

First, as we have seen in the movie *Seopyonje*, a Korean movie about the lives of Korean traditional singers, one must train their voice underneath a waterfall. It is believed that the voice must penetrate and overcome the sound of a waterfall, which includes all the frequency ranges of sound. Just how loudly does one have to sing to go beyond the sound of nature and background noise? Through this step, one is able to obtain the volume needed to become a *myung-chang*.

The second step is to train in a cave. Sound echoes in

many different directions after bouncing off uneven surfaces of mud and rock in a cave. This kind echo resembles the kind we hear in bathrooms. The sound may be amplified, but different sounds mix together and radiate in different directions, which creates unnecessary vibration. Only with repeated practice is one able to overcome the echo and train the vocal chord to release a sustained resonance that produces clear sounds—and thus get closer to becoming a *myung-chang*.

The next step is to train the ears to hear one's own voice clearly. In *Seopyonje*, there is a scene in which a singer is singing in the middle of the crowded open market. The singer

A scene from the *Pansori* performance

is unable to draw attention from people at first, but soon overcomes the noise made by the crowd and releasing tones that overpower the noise from people around her. Shouting, arguing, animal cries, vehicle noises, and other sounds are considered colored noise when they are all mixed together. When you speak over this noise and produce sound that pierces through colored noise, you are a step closer to finding the unique voice of a *myung-chang*.

The final step of training takes place on open land. The human voice on a prairie becomes insignificant because sound doesn't bounce back to us. This is especially the case on a beach with the never-ending sound of sea waves. Also, when wind blows in an open area, one's voice dissipates. When one can produce a unique sound and sustain it for a long period of time, and make it spread with the wind, one is qualified to be a *myung-chang*.

We have discussed the four steps to becoming a *myung-chang*. There is no way to find out whether all the old *myung-chang*s actually went through these stages, but it is worth noting that they likely could not have sung the way they did without this training, which may seem unorthodox, yet is nevertheless scientific. Perhaps that is why we often find ourselves amazed at the performances of a *myung-chang* and impressed by their individual philosophy of art presented through the work of *Pansori*.

In order to perform a work of *Pansori*, a singer should sing and speak continuously for three or four hours per session in a loud and clear voice

Every summer, I receive many requests from various TV stations to analyze the sound of cicadas. It seems that the sound of cicadas is getting louder every year as they cry through the whole night, in residential areas in particular. Why is it difficult for us to fall asleep when we hear their cries? There are several reasons behind sleepless summer nights to the sound of cicadas.

The first reason is volume. The sound of cicadas may be pleasing when these little creatures are far away from our houses. However, very often, they are found on our windows, bringing to a calm morning a raucous walk-up call.

The cicada produces 5-6 consecutive sounds followed by a long cry

At close range, their cries can go beyond 90 dB, which is equivalent to our voices when we sing at a karaoke room.

Moreover, we are easily stimulated by the sound of cicadas because of the sound's rhythmic nature. The cicada produces 5-6 consecutive sounds followed by a long cry. Each sound prior to the last cry fluctuates around the 1,000 Hz frequency range, which is relatively low-pitched. Also, there is a 0.5-second gap between each sound. We are sensitive to this cycle because of its siren effect. In psychoacoustics, the siren effect is described as high-pitched sound cycling in repetitive fluctuation that can readily stimulate our auditory sense. The cicada's cry resembles this effect.

At close range, the cries of cicadas can reach above 90 dB, which is equivalent to the noise of the subway

Another reason why we are easily stimulated by their cry is its sound range. Humans can hear anywhere between 20-20,000 Hz but we do not capture every level of sound equally. We can best detect when the frequency is around 3,000-4,000 Hz. The sound of the cicada ranges between 2,500 Hz to 5,500 Hz, allowing our ears to clearly capture their cry. Actually, their cry is around 60 dB from afar, but it feels like what we're hearing is closer to 80 dB because of the siren effect. The sound in this amplitude is equivalent to the noise produced by a crowd at a subway station.

The cicada's cry resembles the siren effect, with high-pitched sounds cycling in repetitive fluctuation

In addition, the sound created by these little creatures produces something called modulated sound. Modulated sound is the propagation of sound via air molecules that stimulates our brain to produce beta waves. When we are at rest, the brain produces alpha waves ranging from 8-12 Hz. Beta waves are above 16 Hz and produced when our brain is active. The final sound that the cicada makes in its cry cycle shifts the frequency range by around 24 Hz. This distortion triggers our brains to produce beta waves.

There is one more interesting point worth mentioning about the cicada sound. In spite of the seemingly uniform production of sound, the cry contains some unstable noises that resemble the sounds we hear when we scratch a blackboard with our fingers. These noises will wake us up in the middle of the night and may create unsettled mental state.

Then, why exactly do cicadas cry at night? And why does it seem that they cry louder in the evening? There are three reasons to explain this phenomenon. First, the bright lights in cities confuse the creatures between nighttime and daytime. Second, cities tend to be quieter at night than during the day, allowing sound to spread more extensively. Lastly, temperature affects the speed of sound above the ground. During the daytime, the sound spreads in more directions because the temperature is higher. Higher temperatures expand the volume of air molecules, which in turn causes sounds to decrease in volume. On the other hand, cooler temperatures at night shrink air molecules, and consequently cause sound to travel more effectively.

So, here is a summary of why we can't fall asleep when cicadas cry at night. Their cry contains modulated sound that produces beta waves in our brain. Also, the time of day and the state of their surroundings (less noise) further accentuate the sound. What can we do? We can either accept it as part of nature and live with it, or create a device that will reduce the noise around us at night and have the device installed throughout cities.

The sound of cicadas' cries spreads further at night

13

Discovery of the Hidden Sound

One day, I got a phone call from a prosecutor asking for my expertise. A homicide had taken place in Boseong, a place in Korea famous for producing green tea leaves, and the police had arrested a suspect. During cross examination, the suspect reversed his statements so often, and thus the prosecutor requested voice printing analysis on recordings of the victim's mobile phone. I had heard of the case through the media but was unaware of the details. The following are the details from the prosecutor's report.

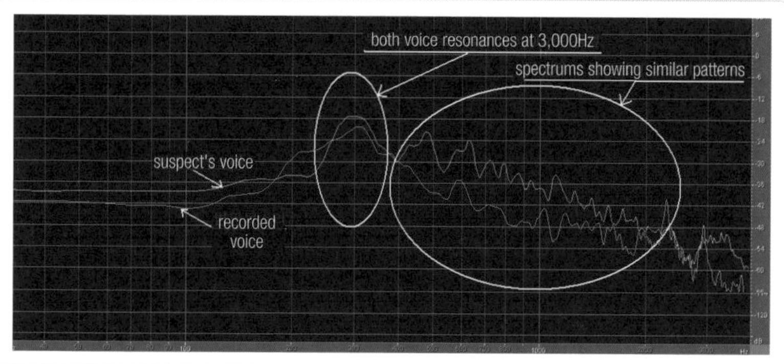

The recorded voice on the victim's mobile phone matched that of the suspect

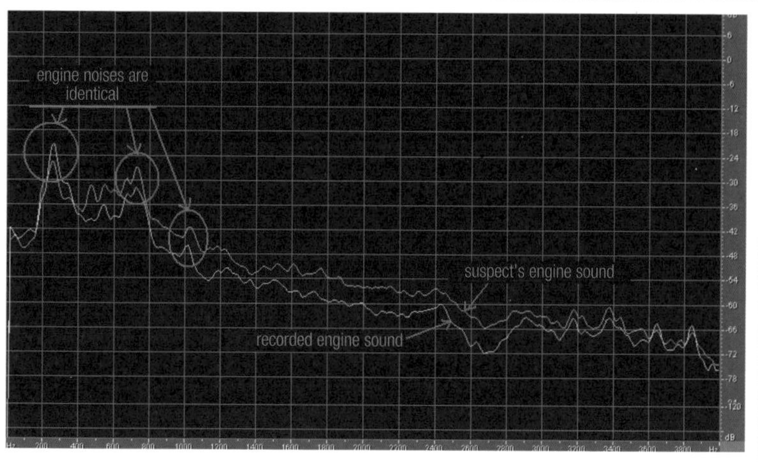

The engine noise from the mobile phone recording matched that of the man's boat

Two college students, a male and a female, went to Bosung during the Korean Thanksgiving holidays. While taking a walk at a nearby beach, they came across a fishing boat. The students wanted to take a boat ride sailing around the area, so they asked the owner, a man in his 70s, to give them a ride. As the boat was getting far away from populated areas, the fisherman first pushed the male student off the boat and then attempted to sexually assault the female student. He tied her hands behind her back, and headed towards a secluded area.

While the old man was focusing on controlling the ship, the female student called 119, the emergency number for rescue in Korea. She made 4 attempts in total. On the first three, only the noise of the boat engine could be heard in the recording. The 119 operator hung up because he was unable to figure out the situation happening on the other end of the line. The fourth call didn't last long either, but there was something else recorded.

As the investigation went on, the police recovered three more bodies from the water near the beach. As it turned out, three women also asked the old man to take them for a ride. He had taken them to a secluded area and sexually assaulted them. The three females fought back but, in the process, all of them, including the old man, had fallen overboard. The old man was the only one able to get back onto the boat. With his unusual strength, he had prevented the women from climbing back onto the deck, causing them to eventually drown.

When I received the call from the prosecutor, it was during the final days of the investigation. They had worked hard on this case, but the suspect was denying every charge brought against him. I joined the investigation to analyze the sounds recorded from the mobile phone of the last victim. Fortunately, the deadline for prosecution was extended and we had just enough time to do our job.

The man originally stated that he had never given a ride to any of these people. But when the police found a lock of hair in his boat, he changed his story and said he had only given them rides but had not killed them. A few days later ,the police found a digital camera on one of the dead bodies. It contained a picture of the man's boat in the background, but it had no conclusive evidence of murder.

The police and the prosecutor needed conclusive evidence in order to charge the man with murder. Knowing that we needed something quick, we turned to the mobile phone recordings and began to analyze the sounds. If the engine noise from the mobile phone matched that of the man's boat, it would be a step closer to closing the case. We also hoped we would be able to hear the voice of the suspect as well.

It typically takes a recording of 10 minutes or longer to identify someone's voice print. However, all we had after going through the recorded messages was 1.2 seconds of a male voice saying "Who are you calling?"

I was able to find conclusive evidence after working on this case for three days and three nights. As people get older, their vocal chords harden and create a unique resonance pattern-a resonance signature, in other words, for each person. Although the recorded message only lasted about 1.2 seconds, it was long enough to reveal the speaker's resonance signature, and thus we could compare it to the actual voice of the suspect. They matched.

Next, we had to analyze the sound of the engine in the recorded message. The man's boat was a small boat weighing one ton. Although there were many similar boats in the harbor, each engine noise was different from others depending on the model ad how each boat had been taken care of. The noise from the recorded message precisely matched that of the old man's boat's engine.

A boat similar to that of the suspect, where the murder had taken place

There were many other pieces of evidence against him, but the recording of his voice that had lasted only about 1.2 seconds turned out to be the main evidence used to prove that he was guilty. He was sentenced to death.

These days, we use MP3 players, PMPs, and mobile/smart phones for recording sounds at hand. We may think that recorded voices cannot be used as hard evidence in the court. However, recordings can be crucial when we cannot find any other evidence. We must remember that even 1.2 seconds of unclear noise can be used effectively to bring someone to justice.

14

I Can't Sleep Because You Snore

Many people snore. People snore because either their sleeping position obstructs their airway, or they are born with a blocked airway. Married couples, in particular, suffer from the effects of snoring as a partner may snore through the night. As a result of a partner's snoring, some people suffer from insomnia. To make matters worse, the noise can penetrate walls and torment neighbors. As the number of people who snore is escalating, many TV stations have decided to tackle the issue, and some of them visited my lab to ask me to analyze the sound of snoring.

The volume of snoring fell within the range of 70-90 dB.

This is quite high considering the noise is coming from a human. It is nearly equal to the noise created by city buses or the train entering a subway station. The reason why we think the sound of the subway noise is louder than the sound of snoring is because the pitch of the latter is below 500 Hz. Yet, the figure of the volume itself tells us the sound is still loud.

Snoring sound also creates something called the siren effect, which takes place when sound fluctuates between high and low pitches, creating psychological instability and uneasiness. The sound of snoring is at the frequency range of 100-400 Hz, and the pitch increases as high as 2 octaves. When sound moves anywhere from low to high tones, people who hear it tend to feel sensitive and uncomfortable.

What's more interesting about snoring is that the sound

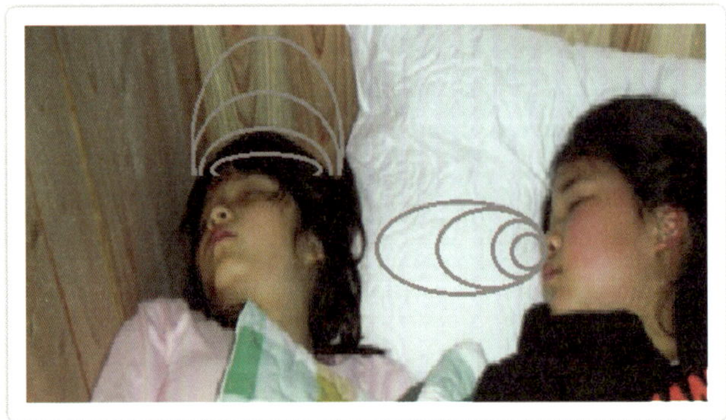

If someone is sleeping next to a snoring person, the resonant sound travels to that person and causes their head to vibrate

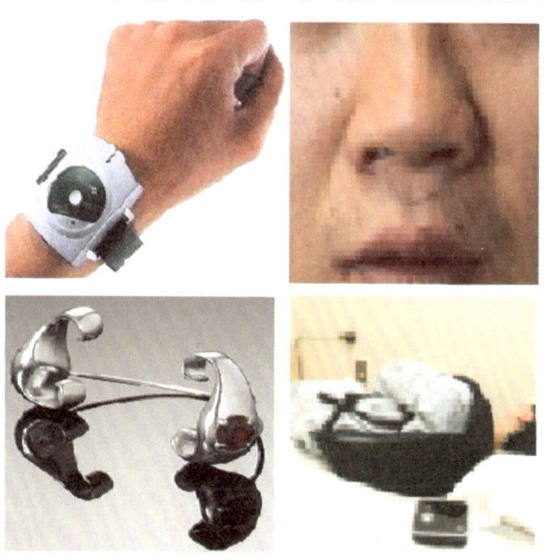

It is wise to seek expert advice if you snore

itself is very special. The sound contains a low frequency echo as it travels through our nose to our head. The head acts as a chamber. If someone is sleeping next to a snoring person, the resonant sound travels to that person and causes their head to vibrate. In other words, snoring "shake" the partner's "brain" and prevent them from sleeping.

Unfortunately, sound within the range of 100-400 Hz travels easily through an average medium. An average room with a sound in this frequency will act as an amp to amplify the sound. That is why next-door neighbors can hear the sound as it also travels through walls.

In addition, the sound of snoring itself is very simple,

but it has an unpredictably repetitive nature. It lasts anywhere between 3-5 seconds, followed by a long pause between snoring sounds. These pauses take place at irregular intervals. When people hear snoring, they can't get used to the irregular repetition and begin to stress out. They even begin to worry about whether or not the person has stopped breathing. It certainly isn't easy sleeping if you are next to a snoring person.

In conclusion, a person next to you can't sleep if you snore because snoring can make him or her unstable. With its low-ranged pitch, it creates vibration in the medium, shakes the brain, and destabilizes the partner in the process of causing siren effect. It is wise to seek expert advice to fix this problem before your partner leaves your side in bed.

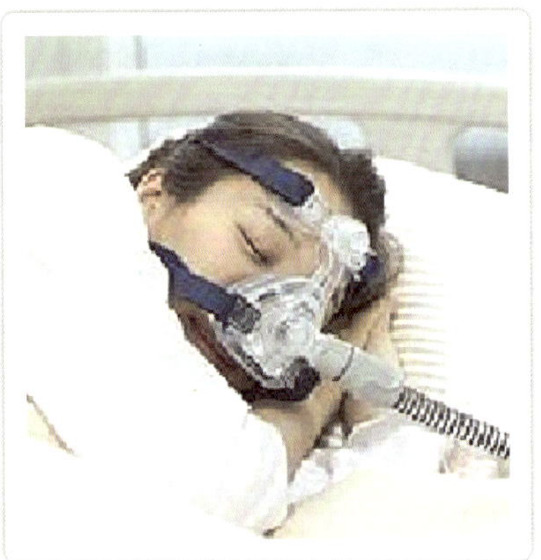

The irregularly repetitive snoring sound makes people worried that the person has stopped breathing

Snoring prevents people from sleeping, and thus people may feel tired during the daytime

15

Sound Theme Park: Using Nature as the Stage

I go abroad every 2 months or so to attend conferences worldwide. Most of the conferences I've been to have been hosted at a museum. I've been to a game museum in San Francisco, a wax museum in Las Vegas, a Titanic Museum in Orlando, a Penguin museum in Melbourne, 6 different bridge museums in Madison County, and many other museums. Korea now hosts various conferences in different museums as well, but I should tell you that I was very impressed by and even a bit jealous of other countries in the past. Perhaps that is why I have been trying to open a sound museum near my laboratory at Soongsil University.

Puget Sound Theme Park in the State of Washington, U.S.A.

My long-term life goal is to build a genuine sound museum, something that you might see in a sci-fi movie directed by Spielberg. In fact, there are a couple of so-called sound museums in Korea, one in Kang-leung (*Cham-Sori*) and the other on Jeju Island (*Sori-sum*). But those aren't true sound museums from the perspective of a sound expert like me.

My sound museum would be a bit different from any other museum that currently exists. In a 10-story building, I would have laboratories and study rooms from the 5th to 10th floor. From the basement to the 4th floor, I would have enough space for something similar to a science museum where people could interact with various exhibitions of sound-related machines and compare different sounds. I always carry a proposal with me to make this dream into a reality, but an opportunity has never materialized.

Money has been the biggest problem. There hasn't been enough capital to find land to build upon. To be honest, though, I didn't really have enough material and data to fill up a museum in the past. Even if I had had the money to make it all happen, there were no specific plans for after the initial investment. So I thought to myself, instead of building a complete structure, I should come up with an alternative: what if I utilized nature and combined it with a manmade structure to carry out the sound projects? This was how the idea of a sound theme park was born.

I expected be the first person in the world to create a new type of theme park if everything went as planned. To my surprise, while web surfing, I did find what I thought was a

The "Sound and Health" Path at Boramae Park, Seoul, Korea

The temporary display of sound theme devices at Soongsil University, Seoul, Korea

sound theme park in Seattle, known as Puget Sound Theme Park, but it turned out that Puget Sound was just the name of the city, and the park was just a natural history theme park. I still had a chance to make my dream come true.

So, here are the details of my sound theme park. The outdoor landscaping will be crucial. Instead of the park depending on aesthetically pleasing waterfalls and great-looking trees, everything in the park should come together to support the natural sounds of the environment and be able to continuously produce these sounds. The theme park's waterfall could be the smallest in the world, but the sound it produced would match that of Niagara or Angel Falls, so visitors would be able to physically feel, or imagine, the sound of those falls.

Now, imagine a place where the sound of nature changes as you do different activities. If you are driving through a park, the sound of a waterfall will be the theme song to your trip. If you are riding a bike, the sound of a river will be the perfect song to your ears. You may scream the loudest in one station to become the next champion in screaming, or sing in another station to become the next best singer in the park. Sometimes, you'll hear a whisper carried by the wind, and other times you'll hear a wood wind instrument when the wind blows through the trees. As you ramble around the park, you will enjoy various sounds generated from nature.

Sound tester to see how long someone can yell for a long time

Professor Bae explains to students how to use a device to test the body balance using sound

In addition, the indoor theme park will provide hundreds of different sounds to satisfy not only the auditory sense but all of your five senses and let you know it is a great part of your life. You'll be taken to the highest floor in the building, and as you make your way down on a ramp, many sounds will present themselves to you. They will first stimulate your auditory sense and then spread over your whole body to influence even your imagination and emotions.

There will be many stations with individual themes to provide the best experiences with sounds for visitors. For example, at the "Sound and Health" station, you will learn how sound can affect the physical condition of different parts of your body and how it can be utilized to live a healthy life. At the "Sound and Serenity" station, you'll hear sounds that can help you meditate and calm your mind. At

The "Sound and Health" station at Boramae Park, Seoul, Korea

the “Sound and Senses” station, you’ll be able to interact with various instruments and machines to realize the importance of sound and the scientific explanations behind the instruments. At the “Sound and Terror” station, you’ll hear some of the terrifying sounds of nature, like thunder, the sounds of earthquakes, and other sounds that are difficult to hear in everyday life.

Visitors will also be able to hear sounds that are beyond our hearing range. They will have the chance to understand different types of instruments used to analyze and utilize sounds. They may even experience hearing the sound through a dog's ear, in order to experience the conditions of the auditory senses of animals.

Soongsil University has expressed interest in my proposal after a couple of presentations based on its detailed plans, although no specific action has yet been taken. Meanwhile, the city of Seoul took interest in my proposal last year and allowed me to initiate the beginning stages of my proposal at Boramae Park. Last year, a “Sound and Health” station was built at Boramae Park, and it is now gaining popularity among residents and visitors to the area. The sound of flowing water and birds attracts not only people but also animals, including many birds, to the park. It is now one of the main attractions in the area with its flourishing sounds of nature.

I am so proud of Soongsil University's Sound Engineering Research Institute for starting a project to capture the sound of nature and bring it into people's everyday lives for the first time in the world. The theme park will continue to expand with unusual landscaping techniques to bring forgotten sounds of nature to people. I just hope that people will learn about and experience the gifts of nature through their ears as well as their hearts.

Water organ temporatily displayed at Soongsil University, Seoul, Korea

16

It Isn't a Child's Cry: The Sound of the Emille Bell

Known as the Emille Bell, King Sung-duk's bell is Korea's National Treasure #29 and has been registered by UNESCO as World Heritage. Legend has it that a child was put into a smelting furnace in the production of the bell in order to make the sound better. People believed that the sound of the bell contained a child's cry when it was struck, as if the child were desperately crying out for his mom.

As a sound engineer and scholar myself, I really wanted to visit Gyeongju to hear the sound of the bell. It is hard to get the chance to hear the sound of the bell. The bell was struck every New Year's Day until 1992. This tradition was brought

It took 34 years to build King Sungduk's Bell, also known as the Emille Bell

to an end because some worried the bell would shatter when struck due to its deteriorating condition. However, some scholars have suggested that it would be more beneficial to strike the bell every once in a while. The management of the Gyeongju National Museum decided to ring the bell 33 times every October. The public can hear the recorded sound of the bell as they enter Gyeongju National Museum.

I was given a chance to visit the museum for this annual event and record the sound of the bell for one of my projects. As I entered the Museum, I saw the bell standing in a courtyard at the entrance to Gyeongju National Museum. Reaching 3.75 m in height with 2.25 m in diameter, its majestic presence was accentuated by the intricate patterns carbed around the body. Seeing the bell, I indulged in reminiscences of the old days when I was young and very much impressed by the legend of the bell.

In preparation, we installed various sound recording instruments to capture the sound. Staff members for the project gathered around the bell along with many monks who had come from nearby shrines to hear the sound of the bell. There were a few memorable occurrences that took place during the process of recording the sound of the bell, one of which happened when two ringers were holding on to the clapper that was hanging from the ceiling. As the bell was struck, one of the men holding the clapper fell on the floor because the rebound threw him off balance. Fortunately, he was not hurt.

Anyway, we succeeded in getting a good recording the sound. The sound was magnificent. It was clear and elegant. Whenever I played the sound, I was very much impressed by its resonance, but I was not able to hear the child's cry in the recording at all! Could it be that I couldn't hear it due to the surrounding environment the bell was in? I was not sure.

This Emille Bell holds many characteristics in its sound. It is very clear and elegant, yet beautiful and seemingly never-ending. The sound seems to finish, but then another wave of vibration follows the previous one, perpetuating a long-lasting echo. It almost sounds like the bell is crying, sad and devastated. Besides being the biggest bell from the Shilla era, this bell has the capacity to produce different tone colors even in a single strike.

I eventually figured out why people believed they hear a

The striking of the Emille Bell in 2006

child's cry from the bell(by the way, a child was never used in anyway in the production of the bell). A baby's cry contains two frequencies, one at 360 Hz and the other at 477 Hz. This bell produces something similar to these two frequencies. As the bell is struck, the air particles must travel through the waist of the bell and pass through every intricate pattern of the metal protrusions on the body. As it turns out, the sound is distorted by 5-18 Hz when it passes through these protrusions, producing a unique beat of oscillation. When babies pull back their jaws and cry, the sound oscillates within 5-18 Hz from its original pitch. This oscillation calls for mother's or father's attention and induces a feeling of urgency. The cycle of oscillation occurs 5-16 times per second when the bell is struck, so people can hear a baby's cry from far distances.

The Bell used to be hung at the South Gate of Gyung-ju, and was used to tell the time to people

But why couldn't we hear this sound? After researching the matter, we came to the conclusion that it was the clapper affecting the sound quality of the bell. According to the museum's records, the clapper has been used since the 16th century. With natural weathering and beating, every strike damaged the wood and distorted its original form. Its sister clapper in Seoul, which belongs to the Boshin-gak Bell, has a diameter of 80 cm but this one has a diameter of 20 cm at the strike zone. As it reduces in size, it also decreases in weight, and not enough force is carried to the bell. This also explains why the ringer bounced back and fell.

Since I couldn't reproduce the sound of a baby's cry, I decided to look for old recordings of the Emille Bell. The oldest one I found on the Internet was recorded in 1966. I had to use a computer to clear residual noise. The sound was very different from that of the current recording, and I was able to hear the oscillation that resembled a baby's cry. It was very impressive.

Some students who have heard the bell say it sounds different on a rainy day than on a bright, sunny day. On the one hand, they said the echo lasts longer on a rainy day. On the other hand, the sound is powerful and almost cheerful on a sunny day. If you want to experience the sound, you can visit Boramae Park in Seoul as we have installed a machine to play the recorded sound of the Emille Bell.

Nonetheless, I am sad to say that we cannot reproduce the original sound of the Emille Bell at this time. It is understandable that the museum is afraid of harming this national treasure. However, they should not forget that it must be struck in order for its spirit to be retained. Furthermore, a new clapper that can match the caliber of the bell must be made in order to allow its grandiose legacy to continue.

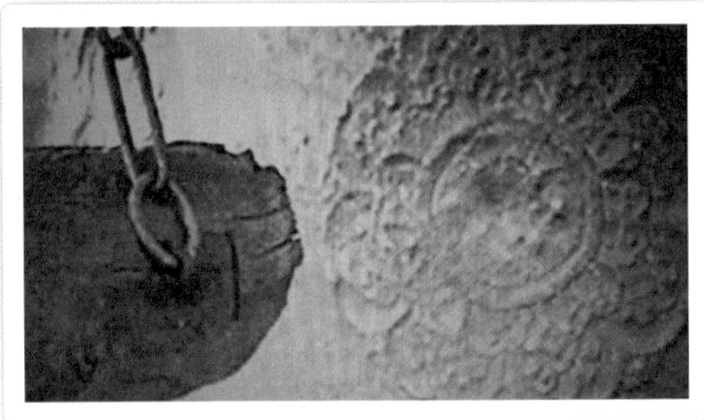

The surface of the Bell has been damaged a lot

Spiritual people who like to meditate seem to let fall all the worries in the universe from off their shoulders. Their meditation takes place in nature, and time isn't an issue for them. They soak themselves in the sounds of streams, wind, rain, ocean waves, and waterfalls, which captures their mind and soul. Sometimes, these people even place themselves in harm's way to find that perfect spot to meditate. What is it about these sounds that mesmerizes these spiritual followers?

Simply put, the sounds of nature are mostly comprised of white noise. White noise contains all sound ranges that

Water fountains create white noise

are audible to our ears. The collection of these sounds is just a static background noise. In other words, it contains every sound around us but does not hold any meaning, and it creates a sense of comfort because of the sounds' ubiquitous nature.

You can easily hear such noises in everyday life. Take, for example, a showerhead. When water comes out of it, the sound resembles that of a waterfall. People can relate to this sound, and so they feel refreshed after a shower. When individual water droplets hit the ground, a wide range of sounds combine to create white noise.

To test how white noise affects people, I have conducted a small test in an office setting. I turned on white noise at a low volume in an office without letting anyone know. Moments later, I saw that people were working harder and more focused than before. When the noise was turned off, the office began to get louder and people's concentration levels dropped. White noise may be very important for people who meditate, but I realized that it is also important for all of us in our daily lives.

The sound of wind produced by an air conditioning device can also act as white noise and comfort people. The sound of the wind can be heard all around us. The presence of a sound that feels familiar to everyone can be used as a comforting factor in an office setting and help people concentrate on their work.

It seems like humans aren't the only ones in favor of white noise. Not too long ago, a producer from a TV station called and told me of a dog that turns on the shower and listens to the sound of it. On footage he provided, I

While taking a shower, you can hear whte noise

Puppies listening to sounds

saw a dog next to a running shower listening to the sound. It looked like the dog was thinking or mediating. In disbelief, I asked whether the dog liked to take showers or not. The owner told me that the dog hates taking showers. This led me to the conclusion that I had found a dog that liked to listen to white noise!

Humans can hear up to 20,000 Hz, but dog's hearing range is higher than humans. The sound from the shower-head has a wide range of sounds, and dogs are able to hear up to 50,000 Hz of white noise. It must be refreshing to hear something at this range of sound. We will never know what the dog was thinking while listening to the running shower, but we do know it was enjoying the sound of the water coming out of the shower head.

We are surrounded by white noise, and it plays endlessly. It creates the feeling of comfort and relieves anxiety. It shouldn't be hard to find a good source of white noise if we take a close look around us. So, why not try? We may start with what the dog experienced in the bathroom with a running shower at night.

White noise helps people concentrate better on their work

Some time agao, a Japanese TV station claimed that they could reproduce the voices of deceased people. They used various voices of men and women to reproduce the voices of Michelangelo and Mona Lisa. After a while, I started to get phone calls from TV stations in Korea to reproduce the voices of famous historical figures in Korea: King Sejong the Great, General Yi, Soon-shin, Shin, Saimdang(the mother of Yul-gok, one of the greatest scholars in Korea), and Yoo, Kwan-Soon(an independence activist).

There were a couple of things I needed in order to repro-

The portrait of King Sejong the Great
The voice of a deceased person can be reproduced based on their body structure

duce their voices. First and foremost, I had to get detailed information about their body structures. The size of their frame, the thickness of their neck, the shape of their skull, the shape of their mouth, and others details were needed in order to accurately reproduce their voices. However, it was no easy task to get these details. These historical figures are more than centuries old, not to mention among the greatest people in the history of Korea. Who would dare guess the chest size of King Sejong and let it be known to the public? Although we have a good drawing of him on our currency bills, it was not possible to get the entire physique from a drawing on paper.

The case of General Yi, Soon-shin was a difficult one as well. Although there are a couple of statues of him in front of Kwang-hwa Moon and Hyun-choong Sa (the tomb of Yi,

Soon-shin), none of them were similar to each other. Even as he was dying on a battlefield, he ordered his close commanders to hide his condition from the rest of soldiers. No one took a close look at him. There are many records of his appearance, but they proved insufficient. The same was also true of Shin Saimdang as no one had taken particular interest in her physique.

Fortunately, we found some records that described Yoo, Kwan-Soon's physique. Elaborately detailed pictures of her were taken at Seodaemun Prison Hall when she was arrested. She was imprisoned because she fought for Korea's freedom as the leader of the March First Independence Movement in 1919 after she witnessed the killing of her mother by a Japanese soldier. She was 170 cm tall at the time the pictures were taken. She was a very tall woman in her time. She had

The birth place of the patriotic martyr, Yoo, Kwan-soon

a pointy nose, a big mouth, and a thick neck. From the pictures, I speculated that she must have had a loud and commanding voice.

The portrait of Yoo, Kwan-soon, taken at the time of her imprisonment at Seodaemun Prison

After the initial research on Yoo's physique, we went out and asked approximately 350 female students to say "I am Yoo, Kwan-Soon" and recorded them. We were able to narrow the sample down to 15 who resembled her physique and asked them to visit my lab for further recording and testing. 5 students were chosen, and their voiceprints were collected.

Although the body structure decides how the voice will sound, the vocal apparatus changes the way the voice is transmitted through the air and controls its pitch and volume. In order to accurately portray her voice, we collected dialogue transcripts from her imprisonment and her trial. In addition, to capture her Choong-chung Province dialect, we went to different oratory academies in the province and recorded various voices.

Using the students' voiceprints as the platform, we combined the voices of the students and the analyzed collection of the dialect. The resulting voice was, indeed, resonating and commanding, but we needed to double-check in order to verify that this voice was similar to Yoo, Kwan-Soon before making it available to the public. The producer I mentioned before accompanied me to visit Yoo, Kwan-Soon's younger brother. He was alive, but due to his old age, he couldn't understand what we said. We had to find another way to do the job. Finally, we were able to track down Yoo's friend, Nam, Dong-soon, and check Yoo's voice with her. The friend said, "Yes, it sounds very similar. Her voice was clear and commanding just like this!"

We decided to verify it one more time before announcing completion of the project to the public. The producer took the reproduced voice to Yoo's only surviving descendant, her niece. We recorded the niece's voice and compared the two voices. It turned out that the voiceprints were very similar to each other. Voice printing works similar to genetics as certain characteristics are inherited from generation to generation. After finalizing the voice as a good match, we sent the file to the Yoo Kwan-Soon Memorial Hall. They say it is being played for people who want to hear her voice today.

We have learned that it is possible to more or less reproduce the voice of a deceased person if certain information is available: relatively accurate records of their physique and the voices of their descendants. You cannot be sure if your voice will be wanted for reproduction in the future if you become a word famous figure. Keep a record of your physique somewhere, and remember that your family members' voices could be used to bring your voice back to life.

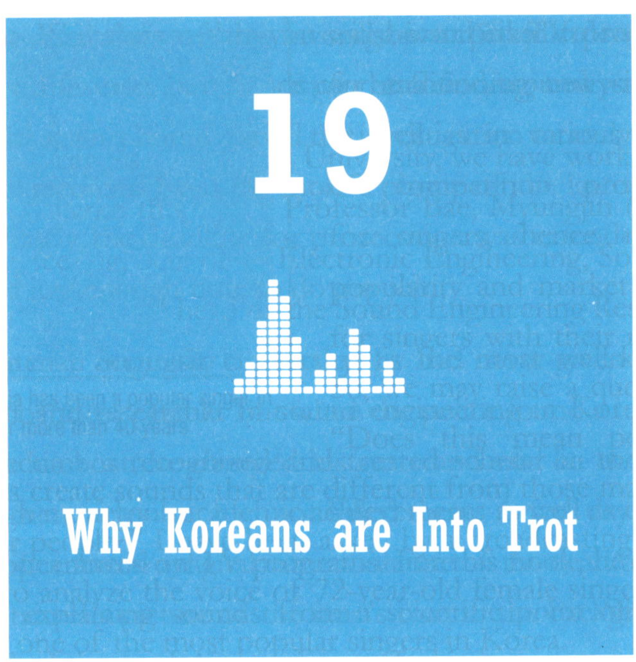

19 Why Koreans are Into Trot

Trot is a popular genre of music in Korea. It has the time signature of a 4/4 beat that makes everyone nod their head and shake their shoulders to the rhythm as they listen. Many musicians say that trot invokes sad feelings, reminding us of memories of tragedy and sorrow experienced in the history of Korea.

Trot is the most popular genre of songs sung at singing rooms in Korea (The image captured from a TV program)

How can it be that we get sad instead of excited when the music has a fast beat?

Meanwhile, *Nobody* sung by Wonder Girls, a Korean pop group, is gaining popularity in the U.S. with its addictive fast beat and creative dance movements. In fact, *Nobody* has the same 4/4 beat as that heard in trot.

Leaving the historical and philosophical meaning of trot behind, I decided to tackle the question of why the rhythm of trot is so addictive, and I found many reasons to explain why people are attracted to it.

First, there are 120 counts per minute in the 4/4 beat in trot, and the drums keep this beat at a consistent rate. This is similar to the beat of the human heart after a light jog. Our body remembers this beat and, upon our hearing the same rhythmic beat, our heart is pleasantly stimulated, and we experience an increase in pulse. A bit of emotional excitement also accompanies the moment.

In addition, the genre has a special intro technique, unlike other popular music that depends on techno beats or rap. Various background instruments are played softly, creating a complete yet gentle and steady beat, preparing the singer to sing. In parts other than the intro, trot depends almost entirely on the singer's voice instead of on musical instruments. Therefore, the audience concentrates on the lyrics and the singing style of each singer. The audience can easily feel a personal connection to the music because the tonal changes in the voice of the singer follows the lyrics, and emotion is carried with these changes. Perhaps this is why we sense sorrow and feel melancholy in spite of the music's otherwise lively tempo.

The trot singer Joo, Hyun-mi is good at vibrato (The image captured from the KBS TV program)

Almost always, there is a sharp change in notes throughout a trot song. It is this sharp change in consecutive notes wherein the scientific reason for people's attention to trot lies. This technique may seem like it is part of a certain singer's style, but from an acoustics point of view, this sharp change in notes takes people on a psychological roller coaster. It instantly shifts and changes people's feelings. It may be considered a technique to hold on to the audience's attention throughout the performance of the song.

In trot, the vibration (vibrato) used during the performance should be given due consideration. Most Korean traditional music contains a very strong vibration. Trot also utilizes a strong vibration to give a sense of completeness to the song and convey a sense of mastery in the art. The song becomes personal to each and every audience member as most people can closely relate their personal experiences and feelings to the traditional depth of the vibration.

Lastly, trot encompasses a wide range of frequencies with instruments and voices, creating something known as multiple sensing. The rhythm itself is kept at a constant of 200 Hz, relatively a low frequency. This is the range that matches our biological rhythm. On the other hand, the brass instruments, guitars, and vocals are played all above 1,000 Hz, covering high frequencies. This high-end frequency range captures our attention and brings enjoyment to our ears. This explains why the percussion section in techno and rap music is at a very fast tempo, only without matching our physi-

The trot singer Bae, Ho used to sing as if talking to the audience in a very low voice (The cover image of the album by Bae, Ho)

cal rhythm, so that we may enjoy the song not through our whole body, but through our ears only.

As mentioned before, the rhythm at 200 Hz coincides with our biological rhythm. What's more interesting is that the average frequency field of trot is below 2,000 Hz. In comparison to other genres, this is a very low range. Most children's songs are at 8,000 Hz, and most ballads are at 5,000 Hz. The reason why trot is in the low range is because it highlights the importance of the lyric and the voice of the singer. Most singers in this genre are middle-aged to elderly people. The human voice drops to around 2,000 Hz as people get older. 200 Hz of background keeps up with our body's rhythm, and the voice range is relatively low for people to sing along with. Perhaps all this is why trot is one of the most popular genres in the country.

The last characteristic of trot is that it uses various kinds of beats. Throughout a piece of music, there will be an upbeat, a downbeat, and an on-and-off beat. Within the time signature, the beat is constantly shifting, avoiding repetition and, thus, boredom. Korean people do not like simple and repetitive styles of music. You can even hear this on-and-off beat in our national cheer during the World Cup.

To sum it all up, the middle-aged and elderly people of Korea like trot for three main reasons: The variation in the beats keeps boredom out of the picture, the rhythmic tempo coincides with our biological rhythm, and centralizing the voice instead the instruments allows listeners to fell a personal connection with the lyrics. All these factors come together as multiple sensing, satisfying our mind and soul.

Trot singers utilize strong vibrations to convey lyrics more effectively (The image captured from the KBS TV program)

It isn't unusual to find someone sleeping on a train with a book in his or her hand, I'm sure you would agree. According to research done in Japan, the rhythmic sound that a train makes at set intervals, created by the rails and wheels, stimulates the human brain to fall asleep. I am also sure that there has been a time when you felt sleepy lying on a beach. A steady breeze along with the sound of waves makes people sleepy. In Okinawa, people record the sound of waves at the seashore and sell it to people living in cities, advertising that it will induce sleep for office workers who desperately want to get in a short but sound nap at a capsule motel. Such

The collective sounds of a beach may open our heart and bring about calmness in our mind

The sound of waves can be characterized as white noise

The rocks at Hongyeonam create special wave sounds

recordings are very popular item sold in markets in Japan today. So, what is it about the sound of waves and trains that makes people sleepy?

A couple of years ago, I received a request from a radio-planning manager at MBC Gwang-ju. He asked me to analyze the sound of ocean waves on a beach full of pebbles, which was called by the name of Mong-dol, meaning round pebbles. According to the manager, many people visit this particular beach because the sound of the waves is different from other beaches, due to the pebbles.

There are many differences between a beach full of sand versus pebbles and rocks. When a wave comes onto a shore full of sand, it doesn't create a distinguishable sound as the water recedes. But when a beach is full of pebbles, a particular sound is created as water recedes passing through big holes and crevices between pebbles. When the rocks are as big as a fist, the sound is louder and deeper. You can see and hear them rolling against each other because of the waves. I can compare this sound to something people can relate to: a crowd of people cheering simultaneously at a huge sport stadium. The sound of outgoing waves (receding, in other words) is like loud applause.

On average, each wave hits the shore and recedes in a 3-7 second interval. This rhythm and tempo is similar to our breathing rate when we are at rest, and also to the rhythm and tempo of the delta wave produced by the brain when we are feeling sleepy. The collective sound from the beach may open our heart and bring about calmness in our mind. Physiologically, it relaxes our heart, which keeps pace with the sound of the waves.

The sound of waves can be characterized as white noise. An incoming wave sounds lively, but its overall rhythmic tempo gives us a sense of security. In addition, the sound of pebbles or rocks rolling on a beach captures our attention. I suggest we all stop by a pebble beach and listen closely to what nature has to offer.

The pebble beach welcomes us with special sounds as water recedes, passing through big holes and crevices between pebbles

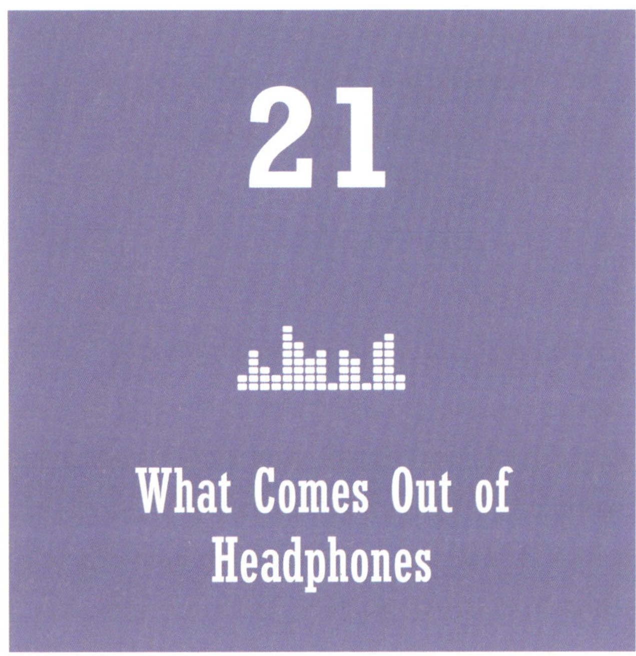

21

What Comes Out of Headphones

Almost everyone in today's society uses electronic devices such as MP3 players, PMPs, DMBs, and cellphones. Most of these devices have a playback function that allows the user to listen to music or watch television. Often, people use headphones or earphones to catch the sound coming out of the device, but they turn up the volume in order to overcome noise from their surroundings. Little do they realize that the sound escapes these devices and becomes noise itself to other people.

Earphones and headphones are designed to deliver sound

to the eardrums. Earphone speakers rest themselves on the outer ears and completely block the ear canals. The rubber edges on the speakers function as anti-slippage devices so the speakers will remain in the ear. But the rubber edge also completely isolates and directs all the sound from the speakers into the ear canals.

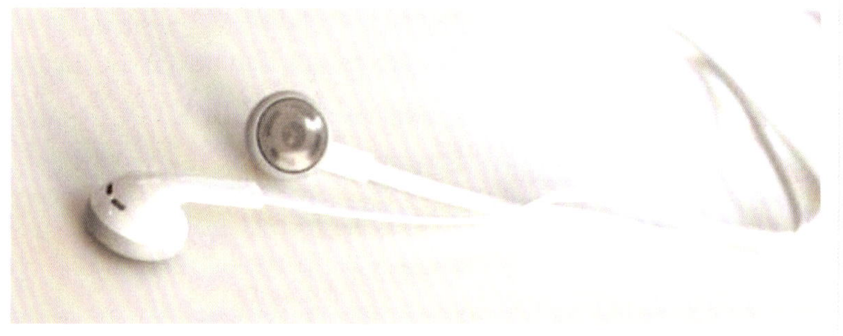

Wearing earphones for a long time can cause noise-induced hearing loss

Headphones are designed a bit differently. The speakers are held by the headband, which rests on top of the head. Because the speakers are much bigger than the ears, they simply cover the entire ear, using a soft cushion to avoid pressure on your head. As a result, some sound escapes through the cushion. Both earphones and headphones have something in common, though. In order for these devices to capture a wide range of sound, the instruments have little holes on the outside that allow some air and sound to escape.

On the sound spectrum, the sound that escapes through

these tiny holes produce a high pitched sound that registers around 6,000 Hz. While the comfort level for our ear is at 1,500 Hz, the main frequency range of earphones is at 3,100 Hz to 3,750 Hz. Our hearing is very sensitive to sound within this range. The human can accommodate a shift from a low to high frequency range, if we use 3,500 Hz as its median. This accommodation allows the device user to increase the volume without much disturbance, but those that are hearing the high-pitched sound from the outside hear something different. They hear an annoying noise.

Headsets are much better than earphones for the health of your ears, but should be used at low volume regardless of their shapes and models

Distance also plays a big role in what we hear. If the distance between the device user (person A) and a non-device user (person B) increases, the frequency range decreases. The non-device user hears a simple yet annoyingly piercing sound. Let's say person B is 20 cm away from person A. Person B will hear the escaping sound at 3,000 Hz. But if the distance increases to 75 cm, the sound range will drop to

1,000 Hz and person B will hear a constant yet sharp piercing noise.

Simple and low-frequency noises from earphones and headphones are a source of noise pollution in public areas. In order to prevent such noise pollution, engineers should come up with technology to block the escaping sound. Until then, device users should be considerate of other and reduce the volume level to below 60%. This will keep public environments pleasant and protect the device users' hearing as well.

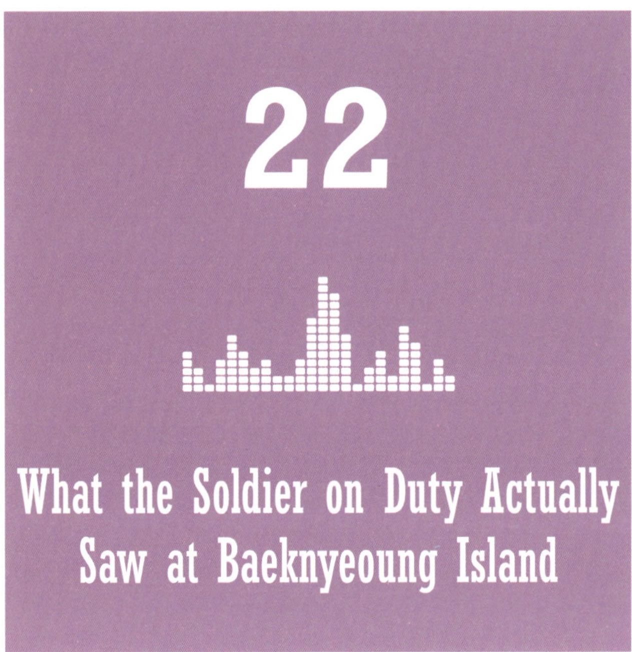

22

What the Soldier on Duty Actually Saw at Baeknyeoung Island

There was a lot of controversy worldwide about the attack on the South Korean corvette, the *Cheon-an*, by the North Korean military force. The event took place on March 26, 2010 off the southwest coast of Baeknyeong Island, South Korea. There were many unsolved problems at the time of the investigation.

Immediately after the incident, the task-force team of the Civil-Military Joint Investigation (CMJI) was set up to investigate the matter. Today, some people still believe that the CMJI hastily came to conclusions that were, therefore, full of errors and flaws. Some thought the CMJI was not fully prepared to answer all the questions coming from both the government and civil groups. The evidence that CMJI prepared to support their seemingly incoherent argument was not conclusive enough, which led many people believe the government was hiding something from the public as well. In the midst of all the speculation and guessing, now at the center of the issue, is the testimony of a soldier who was on duty at the time of the attack and who witnessed the event.

A soldier on duty at Baeknyeong Island said that he saw a huge column of water rising into the air on the day of the incident. If his statement were true, then it offered supporting evidence that a torpedo had been used to sink the ship. Furthermore, the conclusion could be drawn that it was a bubble-jet engine torpedo that had been used. The repercussions of this statement would be crucial to the incident. The CMJI decided to have a second meeting regarding the matter. However, this statement had already created some controversy. Some people believe that what the sentry saw on the day of the attack was a flash of light coming from the northwest, not the southwest, contrary to what he had said. Even if he had seen a column of water offshore, they reasoned, the direction in which he saw it would be inconsistent with the actual explosion site. His statement would bring about confusion and halt the investigation.

Both the CMJI and the public concentrated on the sentry's statement for quite some time. Meanwhile, my team investigated on the seismic activity recorded during the explosion. Our first job was to verify whether the manmade explosion had come from the *Cheon-an*. If this seismic activity has nothing to do with the incident, then we would have to look into a different source to solve the case.

The seismic observatory on Baeknyeong Island recorded a resonant frequency of 8.54 Hz at the time of the incident. This kind of frequency can be observed on a xylophone when a strong shock wave hits the instrument to produce its characteristic vibration. An 88-meter-long ship could be a match as the source of the resonant frequency, assuming that this signature vibration travelled on the surface of the water all the way to the seismometer. Also, the seismometer detected the seismic wave going to three different directions: to the north (N), to the east (E), and towards the sky (Z). Tracing the waves back indicates that the source of the shockwave was from the southwest.

Another incoherent statement the CMJI made was about how the ship had sunk. The observatory recorded a second seismic activity 31.5 seconds after the initial explosion under water. Analysts reported that this second seismic activity was created from the stern's impact on the ocean surface when the ship broke in half, following which its middle part pointed toward the sky. However, according to a survivor of the incident, the stern was above the water for approximately 2 minutes before sinking. Some discrepancy arose as to what had caused the seismic activity recorded 31.5 seconds after the initial explosion. If the stern did not break and sink for 2 minutes, then what caused that second wave?

After analyzing all the sound related to the incident, we came to the conclusion that the second seismic wave was not from the *Cheon-an*. Although there had been an 8.5-Hz residual wave from the first explosion, the second seismic wave contained a frequency of 23 Hz, which resembled the explosion from an explosive device of 4.5 kg (or 10 lb) of

The locations of the soldier and the column of water he saw around Baeknyeong Island

TNT. Furthermore, the origin of the sound was analyzed as coming not from the *Cheon-an*, but from the northwest of the seismic observatory on the island.

What caused this secondary explosion? An assumption had to be made in order to reconstruct how the incident had happened. When the *Cheon-an* was attacked, ally forces sailing nearby were contacted for help. The allies detected a North Korean submarine north of their location. In the process of following the North Korean submarine, they probably made the mistake of targeting a flock of birds as the submarine and opened fire. Some ammunition probably hit an underwater mine (weighing about 10 lb). The observatory must have detected the explosion from this mine. Furthermore, this must have been the explosion that caused the column of water that the soldier on duty saw off the northwest of the island.

The investigation came to an end as this conclusion was drawn with the help of our analysis. At the time of the attack on the *Cheon-an*, the soldier on duty saw an explosion and column of water northwest of where he was stationed on the island. The explosion was caused by an ally ship trying to attack the North Korean submarine, but the ship had detonated an underwater mine instead of hitting its intended target.

The picture of a navy corvette similar to the *Cheon-an*

23 Accomplishment through Sound

You can find fallen leaves everywhere in the city during the fall. Some people are sweeping the street, and some are just taking a walk to enjoy the colorful scenery surrounding them. If you can imagine what I'm talking about, you probably have the sudden urge to step on those fallen leaves. Why the sudden urge, though? The reason can be found in the sound.

During the fall, people take a walk to enjoy the colorful scenery

Research shows that when these dry leaves are crushed, they create crunching sound that somehow makes you feel satisfied and accomplished.

There are a couple of sounds that we can hear from this crunching sound produced by stepping on fallen leaves. First, when the leaves are initially compressed, they create a sound within the range of 8-13 kHz. As the leaves are crushed further, they produce 2-4 kHz of sound, the second type. These two ranges are relatively wide and high. Research shows that a sound containing a wide range of frequency tends to give us a cheerful feeling.

We can hear crunching sound when we step on fallen leaves

Depending on the pressure you put on the leaves, you may hear different sounds

Sound within the range of 8-13 kHz isn't something that we hear often in everyday life. When this sound is heard, our auditory cells sense something quite stimulating. The air pressure created by this sound stimulates various parts of the ear and senses that are not usually used, and it gives us a feeling of liveliness. As a result, some countries today are using this high-frequency sound treatment to treat people suffering from depression and mental illness. People with depression listen to this unusual sound to feel refreshed. People with mental illness listen to this sound so that their auditory senses will be stimulated and they will be more active.

2-4 kHz of unclear sound can be heard when you step on large leaves. This sound may be difficult to hear, but once it is heard, its wide sound range anchors our emotions and gives us a sense of stability and accomplishment.

There are many sounds that are inaudible from the moment you step on leaves until you remove your foot. Also, depending on the pressure you put on the leaves, you may feel either accomplished and excited or active and lively. This is due to the fluctuating pattern of amplitudes, which makes us move about and get a workout. The cycle between the feeling of accomplishment and the feeling of activeness keeps us stepping on the leaves.

There are other sources that create the high-frequency sound of leaves being stepped on. One would be a tambourine you find at Singing rooms. This instrument contains a sound within the range of 6-10 KHz that makes the brain active and gives one a feeling of liveliness. Also, the sound of crunchy crackers or biscuits being chewed in our mouth creates 6-8 kHz of sound. That crackers are easily broken into parts in our mouth further contributes to the feeling of accomplishment we get when we eat them. Perhaps that is why we so often keep eating them.

When the weather gets cold in the fall, the crunching sound from fallen leaves makes us step on them more. That crisp sound is cool to our ears and makes people active. The feeling of accomplishment along with other pleasant feelings is why we are drawn to fallen leaves.

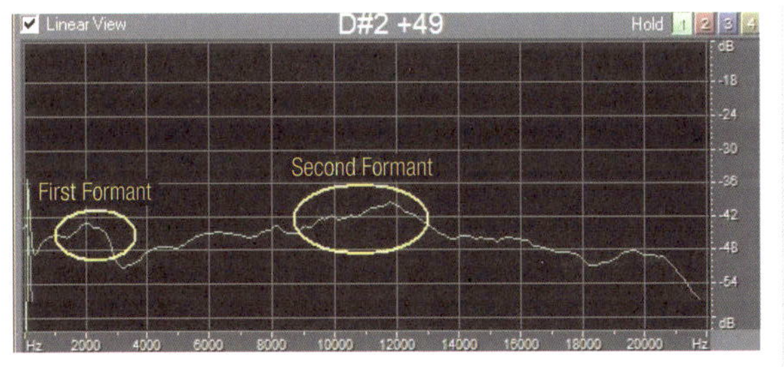

Research shows that when these dry leaves are crushed, they create a crunching sound that somehow makes you feel satisfied and accomplished

24 A Bright Smile from a Beautiful Blond

I used to travel abroad every 2 or 3 months to attend seminars worldwide. I don't do this anymore, but 20 years ago, I used to look at my world map and see many thumbtacks on different countries I'd been to. Because most of the seminars took place at tourist attractions, I would plan to take a break after the seminar and look around the local area. This is the story of an encounter I had at the Discovery Shop in a huge department store in the U.S. several years ago.

The doors to the department store were huge. As I was entering the building, a beautiful blond lady opened the door

A large shopping mall in the U.S.

from the inside and then waited for me to enter first. She even greeted me by saying "Hi." I knew I was not considered good-looking in Korea but, for a second, I thought that perhaps my physical appearance wasn't so bad by U.S. standards. After that, I initiated greetings and even waved at beautiful ladies I encountered while shopping around the mall.

It wasn't until much later that I realized there was a reason behind the unexpected greeting of the beautiful blond to a complete stranger. I was told by Korean friends who had lived in the U.S. long enough to understand cultural differences between the U.S. and Korea that the lady had likely behaved in such a way in order to protect herself. Because I don't usually have any facial expressions when I walk in public spaces, the lady must have been a little scared, perhaps even threatened, thinking that I was carrying a weapon and might try to hurt her. She was attempting to look friendly to reduce the possibility of unpleasantness and getting hurt.

I have tried to look kind to these people and have even tried to smile at them, but my smiles have not been natural. Fortunately, there is an explanation for this. I sometimes wonder whether or not my ancestors were Native American warriors, who often wore intimidating expressions. The truth of the matter, however, is that many Koreans including myself aren't used to smiling in public places. Until recently in Korea, if you were to show friendliness, people would probably misunderstand your smile and take you for a mentally ill person. Koreans don't use facial expressions because of our language. The structure of the Korean language is so scientific that people may not need additional expressions and gestures to support the delivery of their messages to other people.

Also, every language has its own characteristics of vocalization. For example, English has intonation and stress. Here is a funny story I heard from a friend. A Korean man went into a coffee shop in a rural area in the

Koreans don't use many facial expressions

States to order a cup of coffee. He said "A coffee, please," putting a primary stress on the last syllable of 'coffee'. The employee at the store gave him a cookie, so the Korean guy said, "No, I want have a coffee, please!" and this time, the employee gave him a chocolate chip cookie. Stressing the wrong syllable can result in miscommunication between people, as seen in this case.

Your mouth goes through many changes when speaking words. The position of your jaw and tongue, the alignment of your teeth, and even the opening of your lips must change when you speak. Furthermore, different muscles in your face must work together to create facial expressions that fit the message you are delivering through speech. Chinese, for example, has 4 different tones. It requires a variety of stress and tone assignments in order for someone to produce correct messages. It is the differences among languages

People from other countries use various facial expressions

that explain why people who speak more than one language may sound strange or even look as if they are prone to exaggeration when they speak.

The Korean language rarely stresses or accentuates specific syllables among words and sentences. You can speak relatively calmly, without opening your mouth very wide and without having many ups and downs in tone, but your speech will still be understood by other people. If you attempt to speak with your mouth opened wide, people usually think you are being rude and disrespectful. The Korean language itself operates so effectively and efficiently that you don't really have to add any additional expressions on your face besides the ones that come from speaking.

It is true that some Koreans speak with a certain local accent. For example, a dialect from Kyung-sang Province uses unique intonations when spoken, and thus differs from the Korean spoken in other parts of Korea. The people who speak this dialect sound loud and even look upset at times when they speak. On the other hand, a dialect from Jeon-la Province uses relatively fast transitions between sentences instead of relying on a range in intonation. This fast transition makes the speech sound friendly and even gentle. Unfortunately, many of those who speak the standard Korean find these dialects funny, sometimes, even inferior.

This is why people who move to the capital city, Seoul, try to fix their hometown accent and, therefore, can end up appearing emotionless and stern.

There are many Korean proverbs like "silence is golden" and "keep your mouth shut" that tell people to basically be quiet and not speak. If you must speak, the rule is that you had better do so with caution and a few visible expressions on your face. This is probably why most of us Koreans often appear angry.

The Korean language doesn't need supplementary linguistic expressions and intonation. This leads people to appear expressionless and even detached from others. Maybe it is time for us to try something else. Let's try to open our mouths more widely than before and add facial expressions that match what we are saying in order to make a brighter and less intimidating society.

You need to open your mouth wide when speaking English

25 Boilers Are Explosive?

Last year, there were a series of unidentified explosions, or sounds, in the small town of Muk-hyun, in the city of Nam Yang-ju. I began investigating the source of these noises with SBS TV producers and sent reports to the police a few days after the explosions. On that same day, I did further research on the source of the sounds, conducting first a latitudinal sound search then a longitudinal one using various instruments to locate the source of the explosions.

Unfortunately, a false report on the explosions had come out, meanwhile. City workers and a private sound research team reported through the MBC News Desk that a boiler in a building had caused the explosions. These people then suggested replacing the boiler with a new one. However, another explosion took place the following day after the boiler had been turned off. The suspect boiler was not the cause.

The city government then called in a boiler expert, who had been working on boilers for 30 years, to recreate the noise to prove that the sound had been originated from the boiler. He said an exhaust vent for a boiler on the fourth floor of the building needed to be replaced. At this time my team stepped in and suggested that the replacement of anything related to boilers be stopped for the following reasons.

First, it would be illogical to replace any boiler before scientifically locating the source of the explosions. Doing so could lead to unnecessary replacement and leave open the possibility of another explosion at a different site. Second, the manufacturer of the replaced boiler would gain a bad

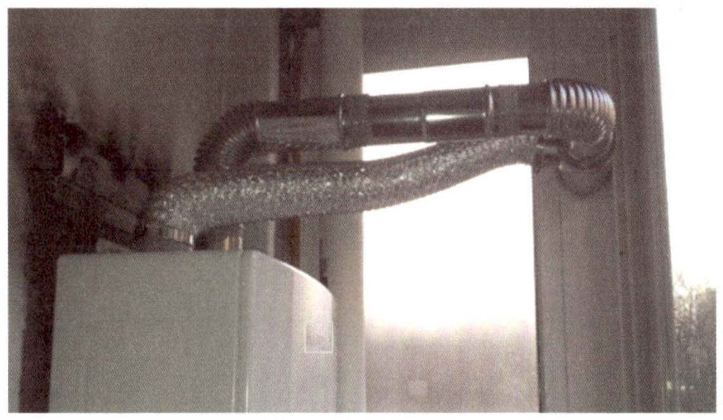

Explosions can occur when exhaust pipes are blocked

reputation for selling defective boilers, which would likely be detrimental to their business.

Meanwhile, the entire investigation seemed like a wild goose chase. When realizing the boiler on the first floor wasn't the cause, the boiler expert decided to point a finger at the 4th-floor boiler and suggested replacing it without providing any specific reason. This attitude of solving the problem by replacing any suspect boiler without specific evidence was certainly not effective.

There are so many reasons for explosions in everyday life. Explosions can occur when a car's exhaust pipe is blocked or even when a pressurized rice cooker has a blockage. Eventually, we decided to approach the case from a totally different perspective.

We realized that the explosions could have been caused by someone on purpose. To create explosive noises as loud as those in question, a boiler itself would have had to explode. But no exploded boilers were found in the neighborhood. There had been approximately 70 explosions in the town since January 24th, and the explosions had taken place at different times throughout the day. In the midst of these explosions, the suspected 4th-floor boiler looked perfectly fine. This boiler was only 4 years old, and all its pipelines and gas lines looked clean.

It wasn't surprising to find that there were two additional explosions after the replacement of the boiler on the first floor, which was later insisted on by the city government. Also, there were no additional explosions even after we decided not to replace the 4th-floor boiler. Over the course of several days, many events, or lack thereof, proved that it wasn't a boiler that was causing the explosions. It was time for us to analyze the sound of the explosions itself in order to locate the source.

We had to recreate the explosion using a controlled method on the 4th-floor boiler. After recording and analyzing the explosion sound, we brought in a standard boiler and installed a set of speakers inside it to replay the recorded sound. Then, a second explosion was carried at in the same way in order to hear what an explosion sounds like from the outside. With newly collected data, we began to make comparisons with the actual explosion sounds previously recorded.

We hear explosive sounds in everyday life, including the one from traditional pop-corn machines

If an explosion took place inside a boiler, the sound would only come out from an exhaust pipe that was connected to the boiler's body. This sound would have a specific resonance signature because of the pipe size and material used for the pipe's construction. This is similarly true of wind instruments. A flute will produce the sound of a C note regardless of who plays the flute, based on the set length of the instrument. In other words, the length of the pipe creates a characteristic sound. The standard length of an exhaust pipe is 90 cm, and its diameter is also standardized.

When we succeeded in producing the same explosion sound in our experiment at that of the actual explosions, the sounds from the two explosions turned out to be totally different from one another. To double-check our results, we decided to play the unidentified explosion sound inside a standard boiler to see how it might sound from the outside. The sound of an actual boiler explosion and this one had very different resonance signatures, indicating they were two different sounds.

The city officials started to cover up their mistakes as soon as the research was released. They should have been more responsible for all the actions taken so far and learned from their mistakes not to draw conclusions so hastily. They owed

Air rifles also create explosive sounds

an apology to the boiler company and to the people of Korea for instilling in them a fear of using boilers.

Still, the question remained: Where were the explosive sounds coming from? According to a local man's log of events, the explosions never took between 2-4 AM and 10 AM-2 PM. The number of explosions also varied. There were 6 to 7 explosions on January 24th. After city officials and various organizations began visiting the area, the explosions happened 3 to 4 times per day. When we arrived on the scene on February 17th, there were only 1 to 2 explosions per day. When we set up 24-hour surveillance instruments, no explosions took place, which led us to believe that the explosions were purposely being created by someone.

The unidentified explosions had peculiar sound characteristics. The sound level of the explosion was only 65% of the capacity of a howitzer or regular onboard artillery rounds, which are not considered so explosive, though explosive enough to scare anyone who hears them. The sound cannot have originated from underground because it did not have a frequency of less than 50 Hz. However, we knew the sound created high air compression because it contained frequencies of 100 Hz, 200 Hz, 400 Hz and 1,000 to 3,000 Hz. The average sound lasted 0.13 seconds, with spatial vibrations lasting up to 0.2 seconds. Indeed such a sound would have been a strong, shocking noise.

Unfortunately, we could not find the exact source of the explosions or the person who created the explosions. However, we are sure that a boiler did not create the sounds in question, nor had there been any mysterious underground explosions.

26 Bird's Chirping, Good for the Brain

On a pleasant spring day, a producer for the KBS morning talk show told me they were preparing something special related to sound and asked for my help. I agreed to help, and we travelled together to An-dong in Kyung-buk Province to investigate a mysterious sound. Dr. Yoon, Mu-bu, a well-known ornithologist, was there waiting for us.

The mystery sound was coming from a very old zelkova tree. The people in town had been hearing a drilling noise coming from it since early February. The noise could be heard after sunset and before sunrise. Unable to see or find the source of the sound, people avoided walking near the tree late at night or early in the morning. One peculiar point about this story is that this early February happened to be unusually warmer than in previous years.

Grey-headed woodpeckers peck wood at a fast rate of every 1/20 of a second

It had been 3 weeks since the eerie sound had begun terrifying the town. When I arrived in the town, I heard the recorded sound from one of the locals. At first, I suspected it to be an amphibian making the noise, as it awoke from its winter sleep, but the time between each noise turned out to be around 0.05 seconds, an extremely fast rate of rhythmic repetition. I thought it could not be a bird drilling the tree. It just seemed impossible for something to move that fast.

Dr. Yoon thought differently. He said there was a type of woodpecker that could peck wood at a rate of 1/20 of a second. Grey-headed woodpeckers are very small and very difficult to find. By nature, they peck wood at the upper part of a tree and, thus, they are hard to see from the ground. Based on the possibility that we were dealing with a woodpecker, I went on to investigate a database of bird

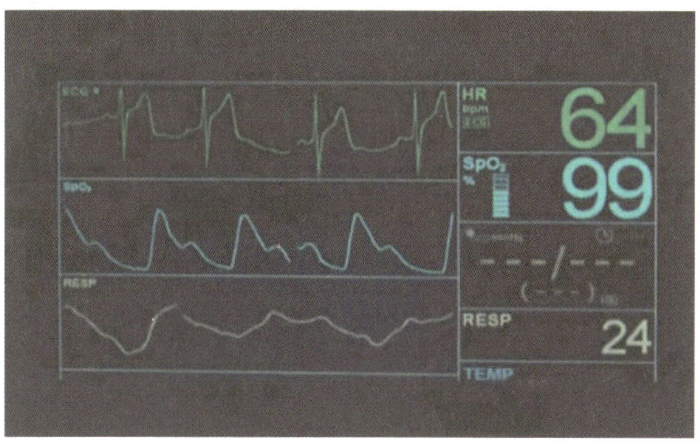

A bird's chirping resembles the rate of the average human heartbeat

sounds to analyze the drilling noise that had been haunting the quiet town. Dr. Yoon was correct.

From this experience, I came to realize the importance of recording sounds to be used for the future so that we can analyze any sound in question scientifically instead of jumping to conclusions based on biases. Edison once said that people cannot memorize sounds very well and that is why he invented the phonograph. It is imperative that scholars analyze matter using scientific methods to get objective results.

Meanwhile, I had received a message from another ornithologist from the island of Jeju. He was asking if I could help him prove his hypothesis that 'the chirping of birds could prevent sleepiness.' It is true that a bird's chirping is rhythmic in nature, with the same sound occurring 2-4 times per second. A bird's chirping resembles the rate of the human heartbeat when someone is jogging. With its approximately100 beats per second, the bird's chirp may bring us a sense of familiarity. The vocal structure of birds prevents them from chirping for a long time. Birds must rest at a steady interval. Also, the nature of repetition creates a huge fluctuation in tone when they first start to make sound. People who hear this sound become attentive, not sleepy, because of this fluctuation. Regular intervals of sounds with tonal fluctuation capture our attention and prevent us from falling asleep.

This repetitive and fluctuating sound can be heard in cities as well. Take, for example, a police car or an ambulance. The sound of the siren captures everyone's attention due to its repetitive and fluctuating tone. Another example is the sounds whales make. Whales can make a variety of sounds

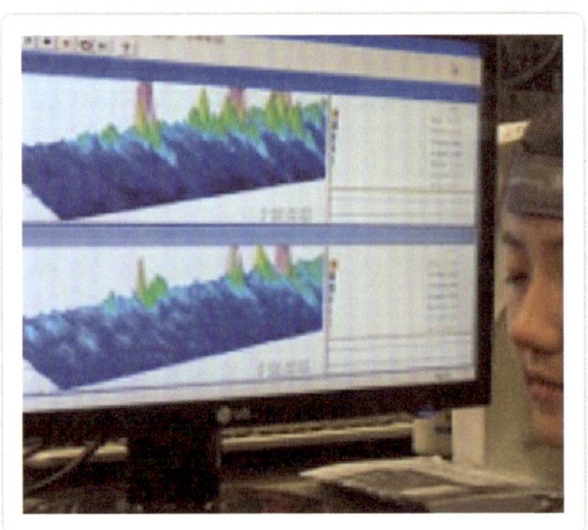

The fluctuating tone of a bird's chirping grabs our attention and stimulates our brain

from clicking sounds to whistling sounds underwater as a way of communication. One study concludes that whale babies turn out to be more active when they hear whistling sound while they are inside their mother's womb. This repetitive whistling sound made by the mother is at 7,000 Hz to 15,000 Hz, highly stimulating the baby's brain. Those animals that can hear at super-high frequencies can detect even the slightest differences in tonal shifts. Both whales and humans, along with other animals, are sensitive to shifting sounds. That is why we pay attention to repetitive and fluctuating sounds and concentrate on finding out what they are.

Skylarks cry at a constant rate for a very long time without taking any break

You might even have experienced this at home if you have very talkative people in your family, or so called 'skylarks.' Sisters, wives, and daughters–female family members are sometimes referred to as 'skylarks' in Korean. As it happens, skylarks cry at a constant rate for a very long time without taking any break.

As much as we may feel annoyed and tired of their talking, we cannot help but listen to what they have to say. There is a reason why we pay attention to them. The Korean language is a syllable-timed language, each syllable consisting of an initial consonant, then a vowel, followed by a final consonant. Because of the linguistic characteristics of Korean in which vowels must be spoken with an open mouth, people have to constantly open and close their mouths in order to speak fluently. This repetitive nature of the Korean language captures our attention regardless of whether we like it or not. If skylarks happen to be quiet for a day, we might even miss their talk and worry if everything is all right.

In conclusion, the sound of a bird's chirping is very easy to hear for our ears because it ranges between 1,000 Hz-3,000 Hz in frequency. Its harmonic and fluctuating tonal structure is another reason why we hear the chirping of birds very clearly. The fluctuating tone grabs our attention, even from afar, and stimulates our brain. This is the reason why hearing birds cry prevents us from falling asleep.

One day, I received a call from a writer for the KBS TV program called *Sponge*. They said a professor at a college in California had successfully boiled an egg using high frequency sound. The writer wanted my expertise to cook ramen using sound. At least in theory, this request is plausible. After all, sound is a form of energy in vibration and thus can be converted to heat energy. However, using high frequency sounds to cook something requires quite a few expensive specialized instruments since we should first convert inaudible noises to energy for heating. Furthermore, the process of setting up the apparatus would take about a year. The

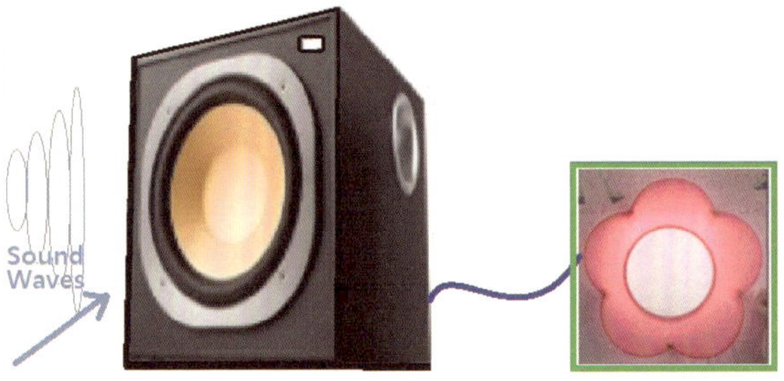

The usual process of converting electrical energy into sound energy through speakers can be reversed to create electrical energy by using sounds

writer was disappointed at my explanation and hung up the phone.

We should understand that it can take weeks for writers and producers of TV programs to come up with an idea that can be used for their program. When they have an idea, they find experts to help out with experiments and possible solutions to problems that may happen during the experiments. However, if an expert replies to their request the way I did, it is pretty much guaranteed that they will not contact that expert again. We also understand that even if we work very hard for a TV program, we will contribute to only for a small portion of the entire program. After considering all these advantages and disadvantages of the project, I came up with an alternative to the writer's original request.

My suggestion was to turn on a television by using everyday sounds and commonly found speakers. However, I warned them that the sounds produced would be extremely loud and would give everyone a hard time. They accepted my suggestion because the primary purpose of the project was to figure out how to convert sound energy to electrical energy and to find a power source to carry out this conversion.

Just in time, there was a science fair going on for high school students at the Soongsil laboratory of Sound Engineering under the topic of 'The Power of Sound.' A 12-inch woofer was laid below, facing upwards, in a hollow acrylic drum with one end closed. Little plastic pellets were put on top of the acrylic drum. When the woofer was turned on, the sound from it would vibrate the drum and bounce the pellets. The woofer was required 100 Watts of power for operation. Having the sound loud enough using the woofer, the next step was to convert sound energy to electrical energy with a proper sensing system. During this process, I came to realize the importance of speaker performance.

Sound energy turned on a TV

A speaker is a device that converts electric energy into sound energy. A voice coil is attached to the diaphragm driver of the speaker along with a permanent magnet. This voice coil is also attached to an amplifier that switches and controls the flow of electricity through the voice coil. As the amplifier switches the electricity flow, it can also switch polar orientation of the voice coil in relation to the fixed magnet. In other words, the positive and negative poles switch positions back and forth and react with the permanent magnet. The repulsion and attraction forces between the voice coil and the magnet move the diaphragm, creating certain waves and amplitudes that send out sounds matching the electrical flow, as explained by Faraday's law*. Reversing this process would mean that a sound could push and pull the diaphragm to create an alternating electrical current in the voice coil and create electric energy.

Our initial experiment was to turn on a lamp using sound. We used a 2-channel speaker system for this experiment. One speaker was hooked up to an amplifier and a loud sound was sent to the speaker. The second speaker was facing the first one, making a connection to a small LED lamp via an amplifier. Every time the first speaker produced a sound, the second speaker received it through its diaphragm and

* Faraday's law predicts how a magnetic field will interact with an electric circuit to produce an electromotive force. The law was first introduced by Michael Faraday and Jeseph Henry in 1831.

sent electrical signals to the lamp via the second amplifier. The light successfully turned on, matching the sound. Now we wanted to try something a little more difficult.

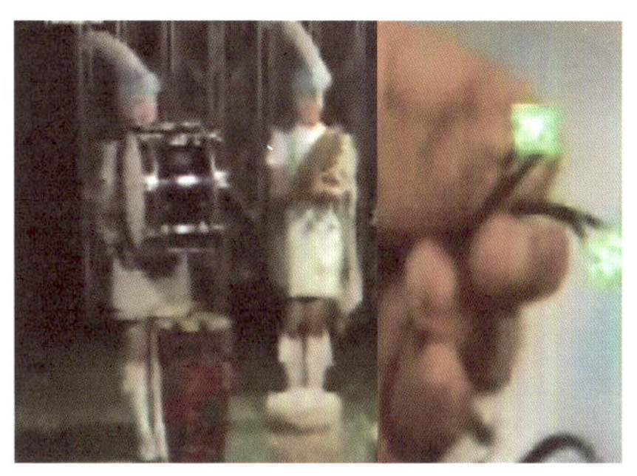

The sound of drums turned on an LED lamp in a simulation experiment

For the next step, we tried to use sound to move motorized strobe lights used in a karaoke room. This time, we needed an audio system that could produce a constant 10 V of power. A regular speaker has an average output of 25 watts, and can only produce 3 V. By using a midsize speaker normally found in karaoke rooms, we were able to produce 10 V and move the motorized strobe lights, which coincided with the sound and drumbeat coming out of the speaker. Having accomplished both experiments, it was time for us to turn on a television.

The human voice amplified through a microphone can turn on a lamp

We needed two very large speakers and amplifiers to do

the job. We requested the program producer get very big outdoor concert speakers. The two of them each stood 2 meters in height and 1 meter in width. With the help of a sound equipment company, an instrument to produce an output of 60 Hz of sinusoidal signal was also made ready for the experiment. The two speakers were put facing each other. The primary speaker was connected to an amplifier and sent out 60 Hz of sound waves. The secondary speaker was connected to another amplifier, which read 68 V of power from the sound wave. What we needed at this point was to create a constant 100 V to turn on a television. We needed a booster transformer to increase the power by twofold. In fact, we were able to get 130 V of power using this transformer. We connected the second speaker to an AC adapter. When the connection was made and the primary speaker was turned on, a 17-inch LCD monitor television turned on as well. Our experiment turned out to be a big success.

Out of curiosity, I asked the speaker engineer if he could keep the power source at a constant rate so we could cook ramen. Unfortunately, he refused the request, explaining that a prolonged operation of the speakers at this power level would overheat the voice coil. Indeed, theoretically, it was possible to cook ramen using sound. However, with current technology, there are no speakers that are resilient enough to last for a long time without the system being damaged.

So instead of cooking ramen with sound, we held a voice competition in which people would scream the phrase "Dok-do is our land!" and the loudest voice would win the game. The highest recorded voice was 130 dB. Later, the event was broadcasted by MBC, and the message likely reached Japan. The winner of this competition was also recorded in *The Korean Guiness Book* as having the loudest voice in Korea.

28 Your Body as a Musical Instrument

A band leader playing music with some unusual instruments came to visit our laboratory one day. He had seen our 'body instrument' performance on television and asked us if he could use it in his performance. Now, you might wonder what a 'body instrument' is. Our body consists of 70% fluid with electrolytes that carries minute amounts of electricity. We have used this property to create sounds by sending very small electrical signals via our body with conductive materials. Different amounts of tactile pressures on body surface area make different sounds.

When a person whose body has become an instrument

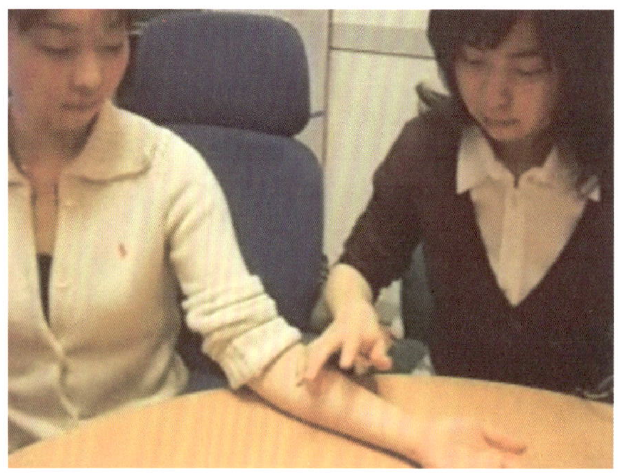

A human body can be used as a musical instrument, producing different notes according to different amounts of tactile pressure on body surface

touches another person, the first person's body plays different notes through a computer as the electrical signal passes through both people. These notes change according to the amount of pressure put on the skin's surface. The "player" will soon come to realize he or she is able to make different sounds by touching different things with different pressures and may try to make a coherent piece of music, although the piece will be simple.

Originally, a producer from the EBS program, *Wonderful Science*, asked for our expertise to create body instruments using conductive paint. A clip from YouTube had showed that a person had painted a room with conductive paint and drawn notes on the floor. Every time the person stood on a

A violinist plays music using vegetables as musical instruments

note or touched another person standing on a note, a nearby computer played the note's tone. With consecutive touches, he was creating a piece of music. The producer wanted to make something similar to what was shown in the video clip.

Playing different notes to make a piece of music wouldn't be a problem if the places for actual notes were marked on the human body or on the surface of things that were being used as instruments. However, without the notes indicating the sound, we needed someone who could "play" someone's body like a string instrument, for example a violinist, as on the violin every note can be found within a single string. We decided to call a school of music and ask for someone who played the violin.

As expected, a violinist preparing for her doctoral thesis

Any vegetable and fruit can be used as a musical instrument

came and played the body instrument after a couple of practices. She played a couple of short but well-known songs using the human body and other things, including vegetables and fruits, just like musical instruments. All of us agreed that we need experts in every field. Later on, we formed a fusion band and performed day and night for several weeks for different TV stations. When our performance was broadcasted, many people found it interesting and entertaining, and thus we gained some fame. Some people said they did not know the human body could be used as a musical instrument. You can find video clips of the human body being played as various instruments based on our idea on YouTube and other Internet sites.

You can play music with a violin drawn on a paper, too

29

Escaping Tone Deafness

Korean people love to get together and sing at singing rooms or karaokes. Singing rooms are easy to find all over the country, and many people are accustomed to the tradition of singing popular songs. Although Korean people are good listeners when it comes to singing, it can be unpleasant to listen to someone who can't sing well. Sometimes, these people do not even realize they cannot sing well even though the scores the karaoke machines provide are not good.

By definition, a person who is tone deaf cannot distinguish differences in pitch when they hear music. Tone deafness can be divided into two types based on how people become tone deaf: congenital tone deafness and acquired tone deafness.

People are born with congenital tone deafness, which is genetically inherited. They can't distinguish differences in pitch from birth. If they realize they can't sing very well, they usually stay away from singing, which worsens the condition. As a result, many such people live with tone deafness for the rest of their lives.

On the other hand, people with acquired tone deafness are born with average musical ability. However, their lack of interest in music and singing retards the development of vocal muscles that are needed to make different sounds. These people gradually have greater and greater difficulty in singing.

People with tone deafness can be further subdivided. Some people do not have musical perception. They lack in beat, interval, and accentuation awareness. These people cannot register musical notes in their brain and thus cannot reproduce an exact sound. These people do not even realize what kinds of sounds they are producing. Other people lack the ability to produce sounds. These people can register what kind of sound they are hearing, but due to atrophy of muscles that produce various notes of sounds, they cannot make proper sounds. However, they have an easier time cor-

A scene from the movie *The Sound of Music*, in which the *Do-Re-Mi* song was originally produced

recting their condition through treatment.

There are many other reasons for being tone-deaf. To name a few, a person may have mental, auditory, environmental (acquired), physical, and/or psychological problems. It is rare and difficult to pinpoint one of these problems as the sole cause of tone deafness.

There is one more problem associated with tone deafness, which is being unable to follow a beat. Some people who are able to register and produce sounds may not be able to follow the beat of a song. In serious cases of being beat deaf, some people cannot even clap their hands for the beat. For the most part, these people have learned to sing without proper training or reading of notes on a score sheet.

We conducted an experiment using the *Do-Re-Mi* song

from the movie *The Sound of Music* to figure out whether a person is either simply tone deaf or is beat deaf. We created a so called "do-re-mi" testing system, for the first time in the world, to evaluate the singing of people based on three criteria: timbre, rhythm, and accentuation. The total score would add up to 300, each criterion being worth 100 points. The score would tell us whether a person was a good singer or not.

Since the *Do-Re-Mi* song was famous worldwide, we allowed singers to sing in any language they wanted. If they did not know the lyrics in any language, they could add lyrics or a simple refrain along with the rhythm and melody of the song. If they were not familiar with the song itself, all they had to do was to reproduce the C scale from 'do' to 'do' in either direction. To make the test more reliable, we asked

In order to sing well, we need to practice hard, trying to be sensitive to tone and beat

that people sing multiple times.

It is impossible to get a score of 300 on this test. No human voice could have perfect timbre, rhythm, and accentuation at the same time. If someone did, their voice would rival a machine or musical instrument, like a piano. We wanted to calibrate the system to a well-tuned piano, but knowing that the performance of a piano fluctuates in different conditions, we decided to use computerized sound (MIDI) as the basis of our scoring system. If a person received 50 points, it would mean they had only sung the song halfway through.

This test uses absolute as well as relative pitch to analyze a person's timbre. Absolute pitch means how a person's tone frequency matches the actual sound of the music, with a measuring of accuracy up to a fraction of 100. For relative pitch, we compare a person's initial note to the same note at an octave higher or lower. Those people who have a good sense of relative pitch will know how to start their first note when they sing the *Do-Re-Mi* song. These people can anticipate the highs and lows through the song before they sing them. However, people who are tone deaf are not able to do this. This means that they will start a song at a note they feel comfortable with, but when they hit any high or low notes, they will have a hard time producing the correct notes. People who can compensate for this change are supposed to receive higher scores.

Accentuation is a representative measurement of how well a person is able to sing with the proper degree of stress for each and every syllable in the lyrics. Each syllable is supposed to have some fluctuations in amplitude. A good singer will know where to put stress and where not to put stress throughout the song. Usually, tone deaf people lack the ability to reproduce what they hear. Also, they tend to stress certain parts of the song but not other parts which should be stressed. If they are able to improve in this are and control accentuation throughout a song, they will become better singers.

As shown in the figure below, a person is given a chart that indicates their scores for the categories of timbre, rhythm and accentuation, where each category is given 100 points, making a grand total of 300. Through this test, people should be able to realize what area they lack in and how their singing skills can be improved.

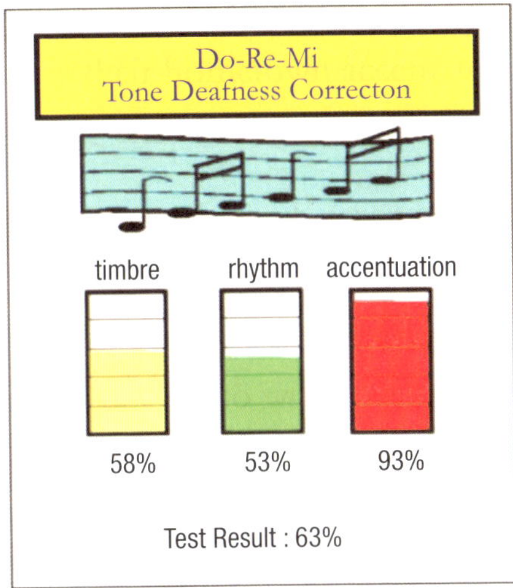

The results sheet for Do-Re-Mi tone deafness correction

I believe this testing and correction system will be useful to many people. It can be easily implemented, and its results are self-explanatory, showing in what areas people lack and in what areas they need to improve. This test can be extensively used worldwide as music is a common language to many different people around the world.

30

What Does an Unborn Child Hear inside a Mother's Womb?

What does an unborn child hear during its stay inside its mother's belly? Perhaps it hears its mother's heartbeat, her breathing, the voices of its mother and father, and the sounds of movements of different organs and muscles. There are a variety of sounds unborn children hear even before they come out into the world.

What happens to crying babies when they hear these sounds at the age of 3 or 4 months, but are separated from their mothers? How do they feel about the sound of a heart-beat? Some people might think the sound would stress out

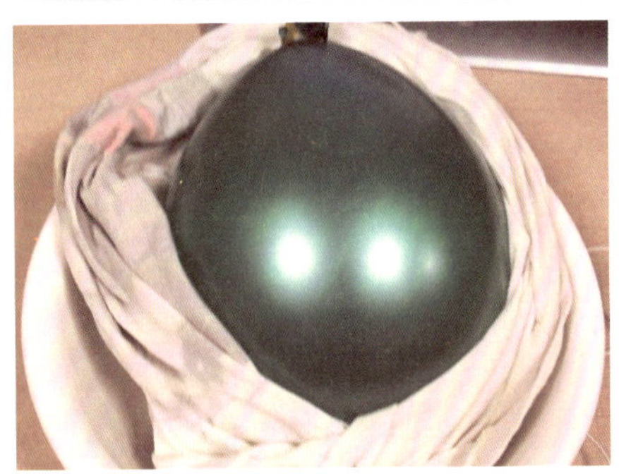

An experiment was conducted with a balloon filled with water in order to find out what a fetus hears inside of the mother's belly

babies and make them cry harder for their mothers.

Interestingly, babies tend to calm down when they hear noise. For example, there is a baby who tends to calm down when he hears static noise from a television. Another baby stops crying when he hears the sound of a vacuum cleaner, and yet other babies behave similarly when they hear the sound of an operating washing machine or the sound of a car engine turning on, or even the noise from a facial shaving machine.

There are many different types of sounds that we hear in our daily lives. Color sounds tend to have specific ranges of pitch, whereas white sounds have unspecified pitches and incoherent sounds. The human voice and the sound of a heartbeat are considered color sounds. The static noise of a television is representative of white sound. Surprisingly, babies find irregular white noise to be soothing and relaxing. It was thought that fetuses had no knowledge of white noise from inside the mother's womb. How was it possible, then, that newborn babies perceived white noise as soothing and relaxing when they had never encountered this type of noise inside the womb?

About a decade ago, I was invited by a television program manager for SBS Curiosity World and to find an explanation for this phenomenon. It was thought that newborn babies had never been exposed to white noise before, and yet they found it soothing, whereas they did not usually find recorded sounds of heartbeats and random voices soothing. I was unable to find an answer to the question at the time. Recently, however, I found some reasons to explain the phenomenon, and I am very happy to share them with you now.

During fetal development, the ears of fetuses usually develop inside the womb close to the mother's belly button. Also, fetuses grow in amniotic fluid that functions as a protective barrier against sudden impact and loud noises. The fluid allows sound to travel at a faster rate to fetuses, and it also has a smearing effect that diffuses sound. Ultimately, fetuses cannot clearly hear outside noises. Such noises are only buzz-

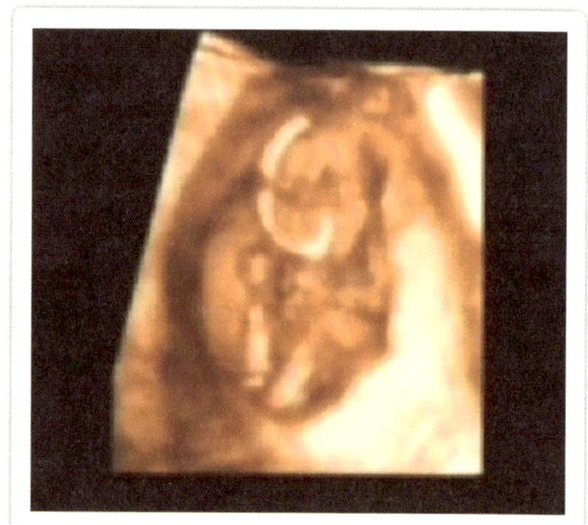

When an embryo hears white sound, it moves

ing sounds for unborn children.

From textbooks on early childhood, we learn that fetuses develop and grow hearing their mother's heartbeat and breathing. It is true that these sounds have similar characteristics to color noise. However, there are some factors which change the characteristics of heartbeat sounds inside the bellies of mothers. A mother's breathing only takes place in the upper part of the respiratory tract. The nature of the human body is that it does not carry the wind sound all the way to the womb. By the time the noise reaches the fetus, the sound has been reduced to 1/20 of its original volume. Also, this residual sound takes place at a steady interval, once every 1-3 seconds. It is only an indistinguishable but repetitive sound from the point of view the fetus.

So, what would a mother's heartbeat sound like to a fetus? The human heartbeat beats at a steady rate of 70-90 beats per minute. However, fetuses cannot hear this sound because there is no organ inside the

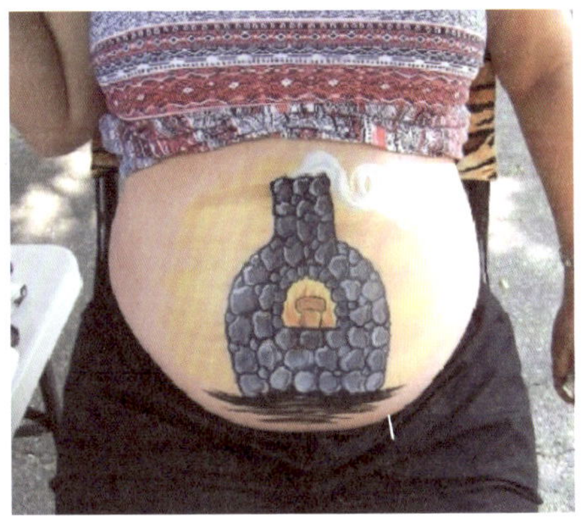

During pregnancy, the mother's shirt rubs against the stomach, creating white noise inside the womb

mother's belly to amplify the heartbeat. The only way we can hear the sound of a heartbeat is to use a stethoscope to amplify it.

Furthermore, different actions done by mothers create white noise. Take, for example, mothers rubbing their stomach as a sign of affection for their unborn children. Because the fetus's ears are located near the belly button, they hear the rubbing sound as simply a smearing noise on a surface. However, since this is a behavior of affection, babies may relate this sound to a mother's love.

Also, many mothers work out during their pregnancies. They usually wear a thin shirt over the stomach. As they exercise, the shirt rubs against the stomach, creating white noise inside the womb. Exercising turns out to be stimulating to both the mother and the fetus.

Almost everyone knows how important it is for a mother to take care of herself during pregnancy, in part for the good of the baby. The stomach and the womb's amniotic fluid both function as protective barriers against sudden impact and loud sounds. Rubbing the stomach may not produce sounds that are coherent to the fetus, but it is a sign of affection, and babies know how much they are being loved.

The importance of hearing cannot be stressed enough. Sound is one of many ways fetuses develop psychologically and physically. It is the first doorway for them to experience the world outside of the womb, as well. Also, devices that produce appropriate sounds with respect to the age of babies should be developed to aid babies' growth.

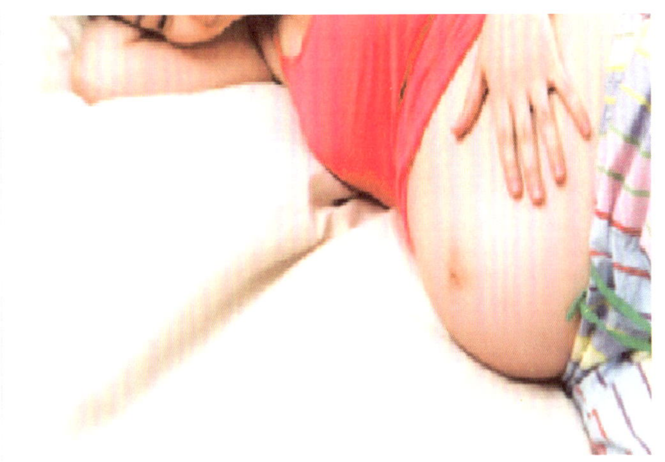

Rubbing of the mother's belly creates a smearing sound, which can be considered a behavior of affection

31

IU's Triple Octave Voice

One day, I received a request from a reporter at *Science Donga* magazine to investigate the reason why IU's triple octave voice has gained fame recently. He wanted to discuss the matter from a scientific point of view. IU, one of the most famous singers in Korea today, is cute and young, and sings beautifully, and is called 'Young Sister' by everyone. She is also known as a triple octave singer because she can produce all the notes within a three-octave range. I wanted to publish the results of my investigation sooner, but decided to wait until her fame had subsided a bit because people would have been too aware of her new songs with their triple octave notes.

It is very hard to sustain a high-pitched voice for long like IU

It turned out that the main reason behind her ability to produce triple octave notes was her lung capacity. To create any sound, we must release air from the lungs and let it pass through the vocal cords. A simple sound is created when air escapes the pharynx through the vocal cords with their vibrations. The range of timbre depends on how much air escapes per second during the vibration of the vocal cords. The amount of escaping air increases as we try to produce higher pitch sounds. That is the reason why it is difficult to maintain high pitch sounds for a long time. Yet, IU can maintain high pitch sounds for longer than the average person because she has a large lung capacity. She is also blessed with a long neck and a big mouth that contribute to creating a perfect sound chamber to hit high notes.

Another reason why people love her triple octave voice is because of her ability to sustain sounds with stability. Many people are able to hit high notes using falsetto, but it is very difficult to sustain these notes for very long. However, IU can sustain such notes without any pauses while shifting 3 times from one octave to the next. She can sustain up to 8 seconds per octave with 95% stability. The stability of her vocalization is almost machine-like, with near perfection.

What is more surprising is that she can return to her normal voice tone after hitting high notes. Being able to instantly shifting timber from the 300 Hz of her normal tone to the 500-700 Hz of mezzo-soprano and back again is something to be amazed with. It tells us that she also has the exceptional sense of hearing necessary for voice coordination.

My investigation into her voice received an enthusiastic response when it was published in a scholarly magazine. Many television programs reported on it, including the main news programs. Soon, the topic was dealt with by KBS's *Sponge*, one of the most watched TV shows in Korea. In fact, they even received an anonymous tip that one could hear what sounded like the voice of Hyun-Bin, a famous male TV actor in Korea, if one were to play IU's *Good Day* very slowly. To my surprise, this turned out to be quite true.

Hyun-bin is a very famous actor who gained fame right

before he joined the Korean marine corps. I compared the sound spectrum of IU's *Good Day* played much more slowly than normal, to the voice of Hyun-Bin. At 78% speed, IU's voice and Hyun-Bin's voice had a 92% match. It is relatively safe to say that two songs were sung by the same singer if the sound spectrums of the two songs match more than 90%.

The parts of the faces below eyes of IU and Hyun-bin are similar in shape and length

As I stated before, the physical features of people play a big role in how sound is made. I decided to compare the physical characteristics of these two people. After comparing the length of their necks and noses and the width of their mouths, I came to realize that each of the parts of their faces below the eyes were very similar. I decided to take this comparison a step further to analyze the length of their vocal tracts. Usually, the length of the human vocal tract can be obtained from a person's height. For an average Korean man, the length of the throat is 10% of the man's height, while that of a woman is 9% of her height. Hyun-Bin is 184 cm, and IU is 162 cm. The ratios of the length of their vocal tracts turned out to be 79%. Therefore, if IU lowered her voice range by 78~80%, she would be producing Hyun-Bin's voice.

IU is now enjoying a golden age in her career. She is not only good-looking, but also a great singer. Her ability to shift between octaves and return to her regular voice so naturally, thanks to her large lung capacity, gives her a great advantage in her line of work. I would say that with patience and practice her future as an extraordinary singer is guaranteed.

The length of someone's vocal tract can be figured out from the person's height

32 Cheering in Unison with Drums

Although we humans can hear sound ranging from 20 Hz up to 20,000 Hz, our hearing range differs according to age and hearing conditions. For example, some people in their 30s have a hard time hearing anything beyond 15,000 Hz. One study has shown that sound around 3,500 Hz can be easily perceived by an adult, while a sound of 100 Hz (that of a drum) may be perceived only if its volume is above 40 dB. Humans have a harder time hearing the sound of a drum even if its volume is relatively higher than other sounds. Interestingly, however, when people are at an event or concert, they immediately react to inaudible low-frequen-

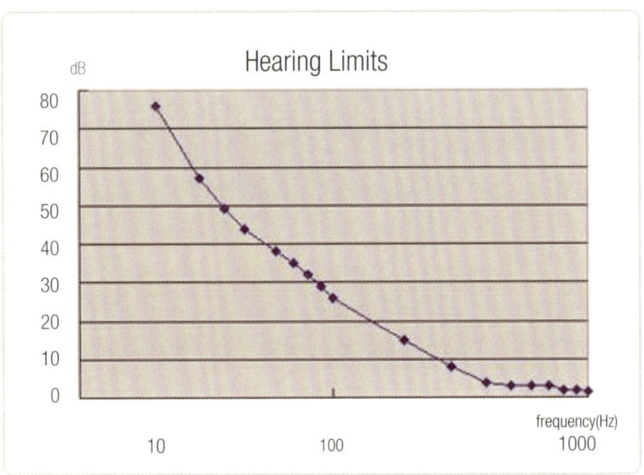

A drum sound of 100 Hz can be heard only if its volume is above 40 dB

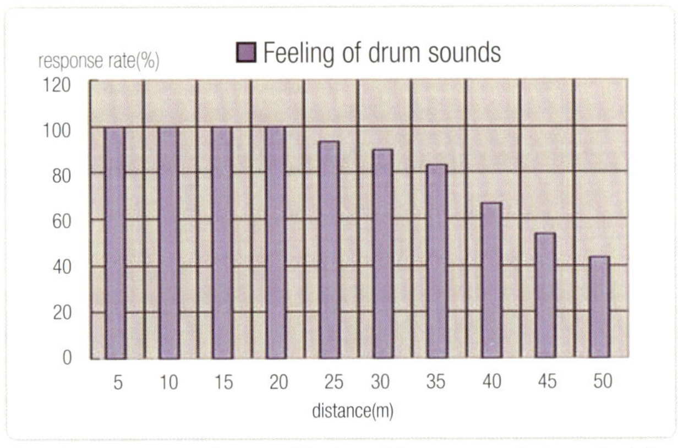

Low-frequency sounds cannot be heard by your ears but can be felt by your body

cy drum sounds. What makes this possible when they can't hear the drum beat? The answer is that we don't hear the sound of a drum, but we feel the sound through our body.

Many people like to visit the movie theater to watch movies, even when they have a home theater system. Some people even visit theaters to watch a movie they've seen before. Such moviegoers not only like to enjoy movies on the big screen and the unique atmosphere of theaters, but also want to feel the power of sound and special sound effects through good speakers at the movie theater.

Various sound effects in a movie or a dramatic piece of music add special feelings to the atmosphere of a scene. For example, the sounds of explosions and gunshots in the movie *Saving Private Ryan* bring a sense of danger and chaos to viewers. The songs you heard in the movie *Mama Mia* took your heart away and left you breathless. This is because these sounds and songs have low-frequency sounds that can be felt by your body. Many people are able to feel them more instantly and more dramatically at the theater because of the speaker systems and this helps create that special movie-theater atmosphere.

Needless to say, there is a big difference between watching a Korean traditional percussion quartet concert (*Samulnori*) live on the spot and watching the same concert on televi-

Devices for creating loud sounds for cheering

sion. Most members of the audience at a concert tend to move their bodies and feel the groove physically, but not many people dance to a song coming out of the television. This is because the quality and broadcasting system of television sounds cannot effectively relay low-frequency sounds to your house.

Have you ever seen a cheering squad at a soccer stadium playing drums? The purpose of this drum performance is to unify the audience and thus help them cheer in unison. The sound of these drums is hard to hear, but your body feels the beat, and you catch onto the rhythmic beats through the

The sound of drums helps people cheer in unison

low-frequency sounds. It is amazing to see how hundreds and thousands of audience members can cheer in unison in the midst of extremely loud background noise, but they won't miss a beat thanks to the beat of the drums.

We decided to do an experiment to prove that our bodies can feel the low-frequency sounds of a drum. We asked 30 college students to gather at a soccer field. Using one big drum and two mid-sized drums, we asked the students to use earplugs to block out all sound and cover their eyes with sleep masks. After positioning the students, we asked them to raise the flag we had given each of them if they felt something on their chest. Drums were hit 5, 10 and 15 meters away from the students. Each time a drum was hit, all the students raised their flags. For 20 meters and beyond, we added two mid-sized drums. The students also felt the sounds beyond 20 meters away from the drums.

For our second experiment, we put 10 people in a small room and turned on a sound of 20 Hz. This is a very low-frequency sound that people cannot hear easily. All the people in the room reported that they were able to feel the sound reverberating in the room, or sense it with their bodies. When the low-frequency sound was heard at a low volume, they felt the sound first with their brain and then with their heart.

The reason why we can feel the low-frequency sounds lies in our anatomical structure. Our ribcage, along with the spinal cord and back bone surrounding the lungs, functions as a sound chamber. All sound is detected by our body and travels through the bones and the spinal cord to our heart. Our body can essentially amplify sound.

In order to test this idea, we used a bookshelf case, similar in structure to the human ribcage, and attached a water cup at the back of the case. At 5, 10, and 15 meters, we struck a drum to see whether the water cup would detect a low-frequency sound. As we expected, we saw waves on the surface of the water at each drum beat.

In conclusion, humans not only hear sounds but also feel them. Low-frequency sounds can be detected by the human body, and in the midst of a sports game with a lot of noise, people are able to cheer in unison following the beat of the cheerleaders' drums. With drums, we can shout for our players together, "Go, go!"

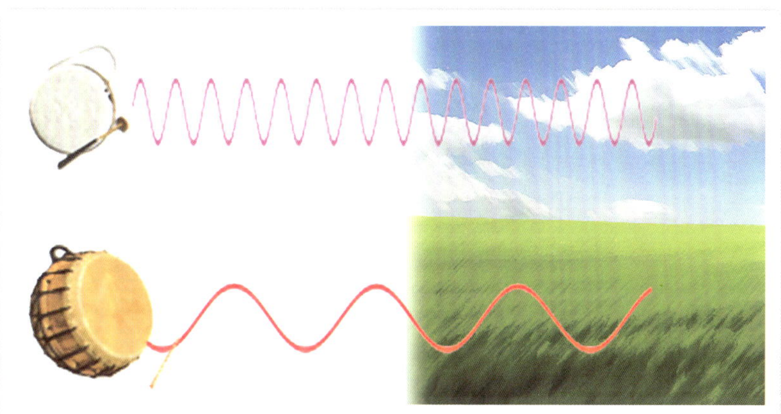

Low-frequency drum sounds can travel a long distance

I was once asked by a manufacturer of potato chips to analyze the effects of a chewing sound on our health. They wanted to have a comparative analysis between the sound of chewing their new potato chip products and the sound of chewing chips made by their competitors. We realized that the client most likely planned to base marketing of their products on our research. Nonetheless, my team accepted the proposal since we are always interested in the relationship between sound and health.

When potatoes are thinly sliced and fried, chips become soft, sweet, and easy to chew. Moreover, the bubbles created during the frying process create a crunchy sound when chips are eaten, which induce us to eat more. However, fried potato chips contain the all too well-known problematic trans fats that lead people to avoid eating them.

Various potato chips are available on the market

On the other hand, when potatoes are baked, chips are thicker, and saltier, and they taste staler, but their nutritive elements are maintained even after cooking. Most importantly, baked chips have close to zero trans fats, making them a healthier food than the fried version.

The manufacturer that proposed the analysis to us insisted that their new product was different from other kinds of chips, including the most sold fried chips in the world. According to the manufacturer, their potatoes are not just baked but they are also thinly sliced, which produce healthier food that still has the crunchy sound, that teases the appetite and stimulates the brain. And our job was to support their hypothesis by providing scientific evidence to justify the relationship between the crunchy chewing sound and positive health benefits.

First, by analyzing the volume of the sound of various chips being chewed, we found that the sound of new the product was on average 5.3 dB stronger than any other tested product. Considering that a difference of 3 dB is twofold in sound energy, to say that 5.3 dB is a great difference is a plausible conclusion. What is important is that the audible sound within the mouth while chips are chewed travels through the inner ear and the tympanic membrane, stimulating the brain and intensifying our senses.

Next, by observing the sound scale, we analyzed the sound in all different pitches including low, middle, and high. The new potato chip was found to create a stronger low pitched sound compared to other potato chips, when put in the mouth and crunched by molar teeth. Hence, the sound gave off an ample feeling, resulting in higher satisfaction. The crunchy sound produced by other products was near a middle pitched tone around 6,000 Hz, while the new product produced a wider spectrum within the same pitch. The sound is comparable to that of a tambourine being hit,

A whale or dolphin swimming the broad ocean in search of food or communicating with others produces the same crunching sound that is made when we chew potato chips

meaning that it sounds fresh and light to our ears, stimulating the brain.

In addition, when we eat potato chips, the grinding sound creates a super high pitch of 10,000-15,000 Hz, a sound equal to that of a whale sailing the broad ocean in search of food or communicating with others. Such a sound so greatly stimulates our brain that it has been used for encouraging fetal brain development, and treating patients who suffer from depression and autism. This sound is easily heard and savored, especially by children and adolescents when they eat potato chips. However, adults over 50 may have a hard time hearing this sound

There were other factors that may have contributed to the

difference in sounds. The newly produced chip was slightly firmer in body when compared to other chips, and that firmness made the new chip last 15% longer. This firmness meant that the chip was harder to chew and that the crunchy sound lasted longer. As the brain is stimulated by the sound of the teeth crunching potato chips, the longer the crunching lasts, the longer the brain is stimulated.

Based on these findings, we sent our final report to the manufacturer, concluding that hearing the fresh crunchy sound of the chip could prove a positive addition in leading a healthy life.

34

Sounds that Improve Your Power of Concentration

In Korea, you need to have good grades in school to be recognized by other people, but it is hard to study well. One of the best ways to improve your power of concentration and to focus better on your studies is through utilizing all the five senses of the human body while studying. However, we usually depend on the sense of sight only, reading material with our eyes. The other four senses are not put to use, and that is probably why most people tend to feel bored when they are studying.

Perhaps the reason why students play with their pens and scribble things in their notebooks is to satisfy their sense of

If you want to listen to something while studying, you should listen to the sounds of nature—white noise, in other words

touch, in an effort to utilize more senses. They also tend to take more trips to the refrigerator to drink water or soda, for example, thus satiating the sense of taste.

One of the most neglected senses is that of sound. Sounds around you can divert your attention from studies by causing the impulse to look elsewhere. As a result, some students wear headphones and listen to music while studying. I have heard that some students today are also using a new form of learning aid that supposedly trains the mind to achieve a sense of tranquility through sound, as well as stimulates the brain. But these methods can result in damage to the tympanic membrane and, thus, hearing impairment.

Furthermore, if the sounds deliver a meaning of their own, students will lose their concentration.

As a specialist in sound, I want to give students a piece of advice. If you want to listen to something while studying, you should listen to the sounds of nature, not to music or to any electronic sounds. Much of white noise, which contains a wide range of sounds, comes from nature. To name a few examples, the sounds of raindrops, waterfalls, and the wind blowing through a field of reeds and tree branches are all sounds of nature that are also 'white noise.'

These sounds are very closely related to our daily life. Sometimes, we do not recognize these sounds, or we even ignore them, as they are all around us. Upon hearing these sounds, we do not lose concentration while studying. On the contrary, we are able to focus more. The sounds may also provide a feeling of protection from loneliness because they

Streams also produce white noise

are present all around us.

We conducted a few test to see how well students would focus on their studies while listening to white noise. Middle-school students from an afterschool program in No-won District were put to vocabulary memorization for a test. Students were given 5 minutes to memorize a limited number of English words for the 11th grade. Those who studied while listening to white noise showed a 35% improvement on the test in comparison with those who studied with regular noise around them.

In the second experiment, students were placed in a library to be observed for their concentration levels while lis-

The good facilities of a library may help you concentrate better on studying

tening to white noise. A set of speakers was placed in front of each student and white noise was played to see how often the students would turn their heads away from the desks where they were reading books. The results showed that students who studied with white noise had a 22% decrease in head-turning in comparison with those who studied without it.

Following both tests, the brain activity of students was measured—for both those who listened to white noise, and those who did not. The students who studied with white noise showed a decrease in beta waves and a dramatic increase in waves related to heightened concentration, such as alpha, theta, and delta waves. This test shows that brain activity is reduced as psychological comfort and concentration levels increase.

In conclusion, one of the best methods to improve your power of concentration while studying is through satisfying the five senses. Of those five senses, hearing can be satisfied by studying with the sounds of nature that are 'white sound,' which will improve your brain activity and increase your concentration level so that you can better focus on studying.

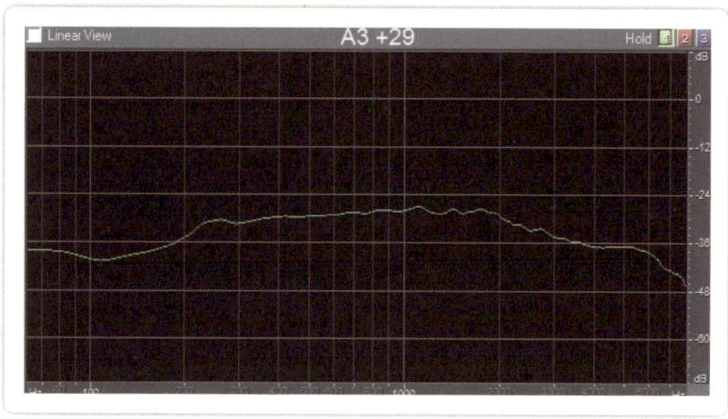

The sound spectrum of the white noise from stream water

Samulnori, the Korean traditional percussion quartet, is a folk music performance composed of four percussion instruments: the *jing* (a large gong), the *kkwaenggwari* (a small gong), the *janggu* (an hourglass-shaped drum), and the *buk* (a barrel drum). These instruments, when played together, create a powerful melody that covers a wide range of sounds.

Samulnori is believed by most Korean people to create perfect harmony between yin and yang—the concept of light and shadow, which is highly celebrated by people around the world—and thus to resonate with the sound of the gods. The flawless communication of yin and yang through percussion instruments and the instruments' superlative chemistry causes in us excitement and relaxation at the same time.

There are also other hidden effects of the sound produced by *samulnori*. First and foremost, *samulnori* is believed to produce a sound that shakes the 3 supremacies in the universe, the heavens(the sky), the earth, and the human, to reach the ends of the universe. The *jing* and *janggu* represent the sound of a middle-aged man and woman, projecting very human sounds, while the *kkwaenggwari* and *buk* produce high- and low- oscillation frequency sounds of 1,100 Hz and 80 Hz, respectively, producing divine sounds that soar through the heavens and are transmitted down to the earth.

In a *samulnori* performance, the *kkwaenggwari* emanates a sound of extreme tension, whereas the *buk* projects a rich and full balanced sound, which brings the sound of the

A scene from a *samulnori* performance

kkwaenggwari down to earth. These two instruments supposedly bring the heavens' and the earth's poles together. Ultimately, the two sounds give off opposite pitches of high and low frequencies, creating a yin and yang harmony as if in verbal communication between two people.

Furthermore, if the frequencies of sounds during a *samulnori* performance are presented in colors, they include red, yellow, green, and purple, a harmony of colors. This harmony follows the color frequencies of a rainbow from low to high: red, orange, yellow, green, blue, navy, and purple. Moreover, in its sound frequencies, *samulnori* embodies all the components a human ear can sense, proving its perfect harmony once again.

It is an interesting point that two of the instruments played in *samulnori* depict human intimacy. The *jing* is considered

When played together, the four traditional percussion instruments of the *jing*, the *kkwaenggwari*, the *janggu*, and the *buk* create a powerful melody that covers a wide range of sounds

cordial and honest with the sound of its overall frequency at 140 Hz, which is similar to that of a middle-aged man's voice, while the *janggu* brings out joy and beauty with the sound of its overall frequency at 250 Hz, which is similar to that of a middle-aged woman's voice. The sounds of these two instruments contribute to transforming the sounds of the other two instruments with their unfamiliar frequencies into more friendly and energetic sounds.

A Korean proverb says that "when the *jing* is played, your viscera become healthy." This is because the sound produced by the *jing* stimulates the muscles of the intestines, which stimulation in turn plays a role in making the whole body healthy. This is made possible due to the fact that the low frequency sounds the *jing* and *buk* create are simultaneously heard by our ears and felt by our bodies. The *jing* produces a powerful resonance (100 dB) that reaches the body through vibration and stimulates the human organs. For this reason, the musician playing the *jing* and the audience within the vicinity can have good digestion while enjoying the performance.

From a scientific view of sound, the tradition of *samulnori*, which has been passed down thus far as only musical performance, should be acclaimed for its sound. If it is, it may serve as a catalyst for an increase in the appreciation of the courage and beauty of the traditional culture of Korea.

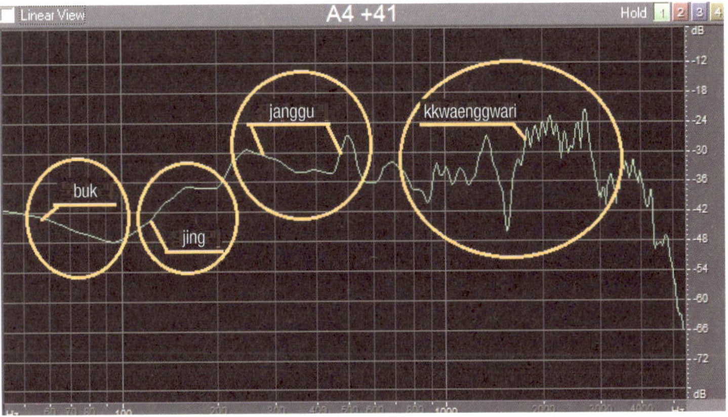

The sound spectrum of *samulnori*

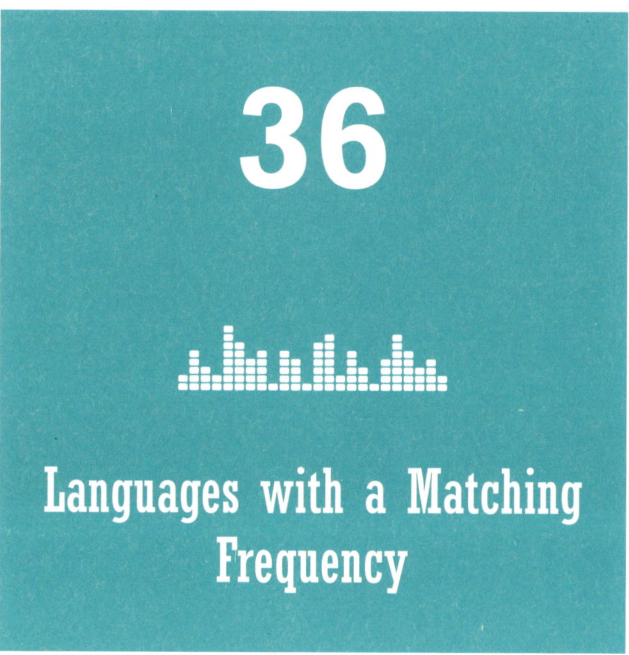

36

Languages with a Matching Frequency

These days, some people say that we should have conversations "sharing a matching frequency." The phrase figuratively means that people should share the same understandings and feelings about what they are saying if they really want to communicate well with each other. There are some people who also insist that Koreans should share the same frequency as native speakers of English if we want to speak English fluently. Moreover, they assume that speaking on a different frequency is the reason why Koreans don't speak English very well even after having studied English so hard for many years. What does it mean to have the same frequency in the

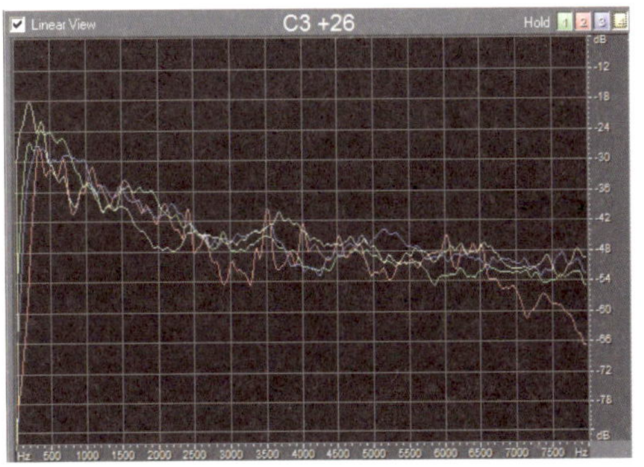

The average frequency (or pitch) of people's voices over a certain period of time is the same for people regardless of gender and age.

case of languages? Is it true that English has a frequency totally different from that of Korean?

The frequency of sounds—or pitch—may differ, not from language to language, but from person to person, with respect to age, gender, and speech environment. A girl may speak at a higher pitch than a male adult. A boy can scream at a higher pitch than a female adult. One thing we may point out is that certain languages may have different patterns of intonation—a different pitch contour pattern over a sentence, in other words—but nothing else.

The reason why some Koreans don't speak English very well even after studying it very hard for many years may be found in the fact that we don't really understand the systematic differences between Korean and English. There are

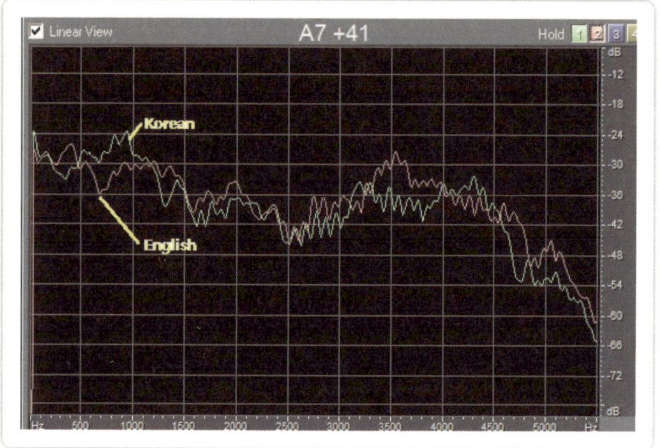

The average frequency (or pitch) of sound over a certain period of time is the same in different languages, including Korean and English.

many students who try to translate Korean sentences into English based on direct translation. This will never work as English is a foreign language having different structures of sound and grammar than Korean, not to mention a totally different set of pronunciation rules.

One important distinction between English and Korean is that Korean is a syllable-timed language, whereas English is a stress-timed language. Namely, the time of articulation in Korean is decided by the number of syllables in a word or sentence, whereas the time of articulation in English is determined by the number of stresses in a word or sentence. As shown in the following example, sentences with the same number of stresses in English take almost the same time to articulate.

People plant trees.

The people are planting trees.

The people have planted some trees.

The people should have planted some more trees.

In addition, the presence of stress may also decide the pitch pattern of an English sentence, since stressed vowels are pronounced higher in pitch, louder in intensity, and longer in length. On the other hand, unstressed vowels are pronounced lower in pitch, less loud in intensity, and shorter in length, making it difficult for non-native English speakers to fully understand what an English speaker is saying in everyday conversation.

Another distinction between Korean and English can be

People are likely to react more to words spoken with local accents than normal speech. (The scene of a comedian speaking Kyung-sang dialect, captured from KBS TV *Gag Concert*)

found in the relationship between a sound and the meaning of the sound, that is, in more professional terms, the phonemic distinction. For instance, the consonant /p/ is found both in Korean and English. As shown in a set of words having different meanings, such as in /p^hul/ (grass) and /p*ul/ (horn: p* is the unaspirated /p/), the completely distinguished sounds of [p^h] and [p*] create different meanings in Korean. Contrastingly, in English, the consonant /p/ sounds a little different in a set of words like 'pine' and 'special', but without creating any difference in meaning: the aspirated [p^h] is said in the initial position of a word and the unaspirated [p*] is said after /s/. This difference in the pronunciation of /p/ does not bring any special difference in meaning. That is to say, the system of relating a certain sound to a word's meaning is distinctive in each language.

Furthermore, in English, the vibration of the glottis is very important in creating voicing of sounds in words with different meanings from similar words with voiceless sounds: When the glottis vibrates, the consonants are pronounced as voiced sounds regardless of their position in words. In Korean, the voicing of consonants is usually determined by their location in words. Consonants are basically pronounced as voiceless, without vibrating glottis, but they become voiced when located in between voiced sounds like vowels and nasal sounds. This shows that each language has its own conditions for determining specific properties of sounds with respect to meaning.

There are many more contrastive features between Korean and English. This is because they are very different languages, from a linguistic as well as cultural point of view. In order for Korean people and native-English speakers to share a conversation on 'a matching frequency' in either of their languages, finding differences in the ranges of frequencies of the two languages is not necessary. So, then, what is most important to having good communication between speakers of different languages? It is to accept cultural differences between the two and to understand unique expressions that have been formed through the history of each language. A conversation on the same frequency comes from having an open-minded attitude in a global society.

Female audience members produce more passionate responses in a matching frequency with the invited speaker.

37

I Say "Meong-meong," You Say "Woof-woof"

In a scene from a recently broadcasted drama, *The Deep Rooted Tree*, King Sejong the Great collects numerous different sounds while creating the original script for Korean alphabetic letters, which is also known as the *Hunminjeongeum*. The scene where the King demands his servant mimic animal sounds such as those of dogs and roosters was not added for mere laughter. The hidden purpose of the scene was to show that the Korean writing system is a superb one that can not only represent the sounds of human speech, but also verbalize all of the different kinds of sounds from nature; that is to say, the Korean writing system, Hangeul, enables people to transcribe exact sounds in writing. It is a great language for onomatopoeia.

By definition, onomatopoeia is a word or set of words that directly express sounds that are made naturally, such as those of animals, thunder, or wind. The word originated in ancient Greek, and means to "make sound by oneself." When people hear natural sounds, they try to express the sounds utilizing their writing systems; in other words, they make an effort to name the sound. Consequently, many people expect onomatopoeic words from different languages describing the same sound to be written in such a way that the final results sound very similar or even exactly the same.

However, the reality differs from the theory.

For instance, the dog's bark is expressed as 'meong-meong' in Korean, but expressed differently in Japan as 'wan-wan.' In English, it is 'woof-woof.' In Italian, it is 'bu-bu,' and in French, it is 'ouâ-ouâ.' For the cat's meow, English expresses it as 'meow,' while Korean language verbalizes it as 'yaong-yaong.' In French, the onomatopoeic word for a cat's cry is 'ron-ron,' and in German it is 'schnurr,' an apparently unpronounceable word. A common onomatopoeic word in English and Korean, the ringing sound of the bell, 'ding-dong,' is once again very different in German, where it is verbalized as 'bim-bam.' We can find so many examples

The barking sounds of dogs are expressed in different words in each language although the sounds are heard the same

A toy company in Japan developed a device that translates the barking sounds of dogs into human language

like these in which the same sound is expressed very differently in various languages. This is because when a natural sound is converted into a written word, it takes the form of a language used by a group of people, hence carrying

Even the sounds of bells are expressed in different words in different languages

their cultural background. In addition, the basic relationship between the sound and the meaning of the word may be arbitrary, with the assigning of a certain meaning to a certain word without any specific reason.

So, should we then invent a translating machine for non-human sounds, one that not just converts the sounds we hear into written word, but also allows us to correctly comprehend the meanings of natural sounds?

10 years ago, a toy company in Japan developed a device that translates the barking sounds of dogs into human language. Developed after a long period of research completed by acousticians and ethologists, *Bowlingual* claimed that they succeeded in transmitting the barking sounds of the dog into human language. The barking sounds of dogs are collected through a 3-inch wireless microphone, and then they go through the main database. On the screen, sounds made by

the dog such as groans, yelps, and wails are categorized into 6 different emotions: happiness, sadness, disappointment, anger, insistence and demand. Also, simple sentences like 'You are scolding me' that describe the dog's emotions are displayed on the screen. *Time* magazine selected *Bowlingual* as one of the most successful products of 2002, valuing its importance in attempting to translate natural sounds into human languages.

Through humans' boundless creativity and effort, including that of *Bowlingual*, communication with animals has become possible to a certain extent. Continuing with this progress, humankind may one day be able to communicate with everything that exists in nature. That is to say, there may be a day when humans can understand what non-human creatures say—not only all the organisms on Earth including flowers, trees and insects, but also non-living organisms such as wind, rocks, water and dust in the sky. Well, aren't we already communicating very well with 'supposedly existing' aliens in science fiction films?

The so-called "Chanelers" claim that they can communicate with aliens. (The scene of the landing place for aliens, captured from Chanel A, *Logical Solution*)

38 The Power of Campaign Songs

During elections, parties use various campaign strategies in order to win more votes. Among the various methods, the utilization of a campaign song, or so-called 'logo song,' to stimulate the sense of hearing of voters has a positive impact on giving a good impression of the candidates.

Normally, candidates who employ the sense of sight in their campaign face more limitations in catching the attention of voters as voters can simply close their eyes or walk away, leaving behind the candidate. However, the image enhancement of the candidate achieved through the use of sound has the advantage of delivering a message afar and in

Voters are listening to the speeches of candidates

all directions so that voters will, even if unknowingly, hear it.

In particular, when candidates use a popular song, the song excites voters with its familiar melody and rhythm and further enhances the candidate's image through the newly written lyrics. Types of music that are favored by candidates and voters in Korea tend to be popular trot with a fast beat, as well as lively dance music. What do such songs really bring to elections? To answer this question, we investigated the potency of such music.

When popular trot is used as a campaign song, voters unconsciously move their bodies to the rhythm. Using popular songs has one more advantage. The amplitude of noise in an election campaign should not exceed 85 dB, according to law. However, when voters are listening to familiar songs, they do not feel discomfort even when the volume is greater than 85 dB.

Furthermore, trot songs have a four four time rhythm–"boom boom boom boom"–which coincides with a person's body pulse. Hence, dancing to such a rhythm has a positive effect on the human body, providing voters with amusement and energy. The human body has an average pulse rate of between 60-80 beats per minute, which increases to 80-120 beats per minute after a moderate workout. On the other hand, trot has a tempo of 100-180 beats per minute, a little faster than the human pulse rate. Thus, when trot songs are played in a campaign, voters sing and dance along with the beat, causing their pulse to increase, whereupon their pulse matches the tempo of the song, which leads them to feel lively and energetic.

Of course, not all trot songs are suitable as logo songs. With their slow rhythm, most trot songs appeal to middle- to old-aged people, which is the reason why it is hard to attract younger people with them. However, recently composed trot songs have faster tempos and are now used as logo songs

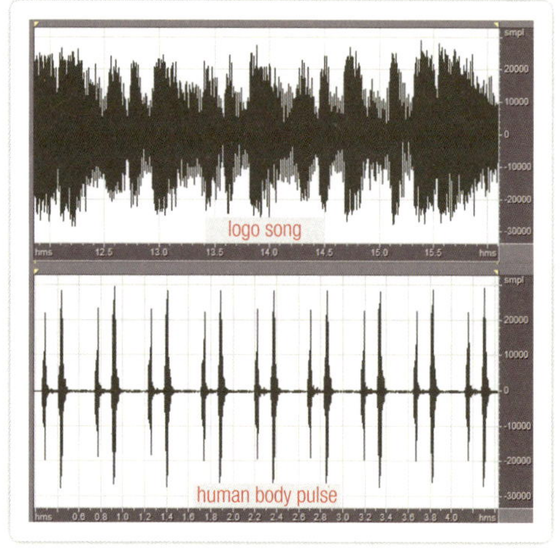

The rhythm of trot campaign songs coincides with the human body pulse

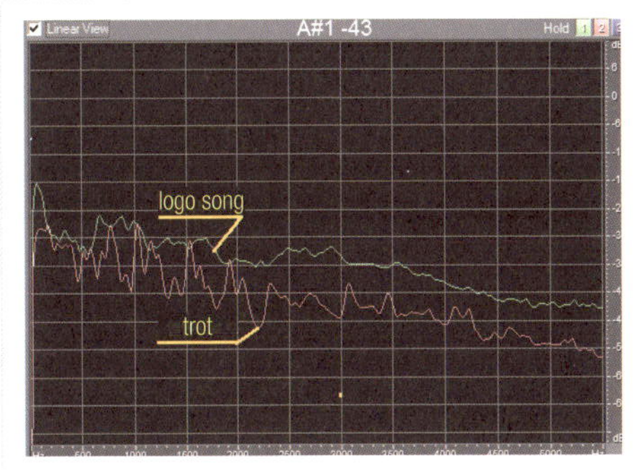

The spectrograms of trot campaign songs and regular trot songs

in many campaigns. Furthermore, most logo songs used in election campaigns employ the complete wide range of the sound spectrum that the human ear can hear. Herein probably lies the power of logo songs to gain the completely undivided attention of voters.

Nonetheless, a prerequisite to holding such attraction is to cause voters to feel passion. In order to accomplish this, the singer must have a sonorous voice and control the rhythm and tempo so that they are faster than usual. In addition, the main reason trot songs are employed as campaign logo songs in Korea is due to their expressive lyrics. Trot songs have a repetitive four four time pattern, which helps voters listen to the lyrics. When a rhythm repeats "boom boom boom boom," the lyrics flowing out with the beat can touch people's hearts more effectively. This can lead listeners to be more open to the messages delivered by candidates. This may also be the reason why the songs give listeners feelings of friendship and warm-heartedness, even after the lyrics are changed to totally different ones from those of the original song.

The main purpose of a logo song is to attract voters and thus win more votes. Playing popular music such as trot songs or dance music with alterations to the lyrics, tempo, and beat may indeed be a well-designed and effective way of appealing to voters.

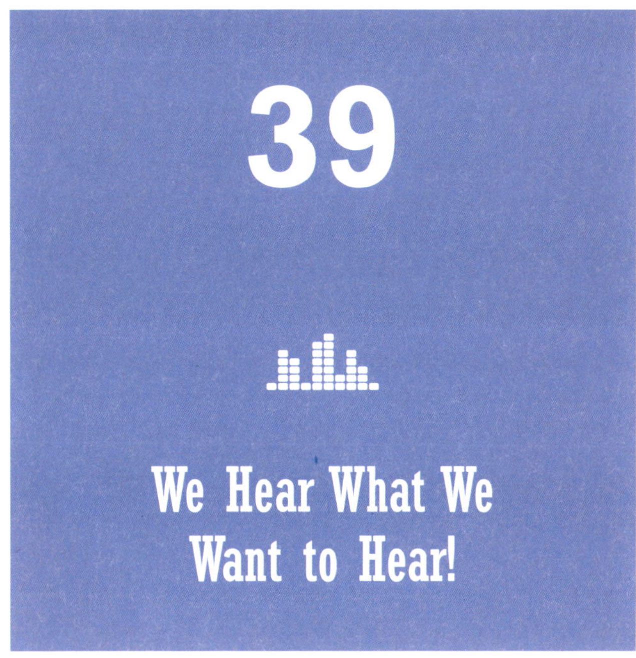

39 We Hear What We Want to Hear!

Complications often arise from people mishearing words in a conversation. It is not uncommon for two individuals to get into an argument due to a misunderstanding over spoken words, and such mistakes can also be seen on public television. Recently, a singer was thought to have used a bad word on a national television program, which caused the online community to revolt. The controversy eventually diminished after our team provided an explanation based on an acoustic analysis of her speech, that it was a misunderstanding due to her speaking too quickly.

Such events occur when one speaks unclearly, which thus

Our imprinted experiences control our language competency and, hence, we hear what we want to hear (The scene of the experiment for imprinting in hearing, captured from KBS *Sponge*)

causes the audience to hear and analyze what one has said according to their experiences. For example, when a child under the age of 10 is told to repeat "Your dada is home," they say "dada," whereas a teenager would naturally say "dad," correcting what they hear. The decision is made in the brain even before the sound is heard, based on the accumulated experiences of the listener. This is known as "imprints from previous experiences."

Seeing works faster than hearing for imprinting experiences (The scene of the experiment for imprinting speed of seeing compared to that of hearing, captured from KBS *Sponge*)

The effects of imprinting have received much attention as an interesting phenomenon in everyday life. As previously broadcasted in a television program, the average clucking of a chicken can sound like "*Sun Saeng Nim*" ('teacher') when a chicken is heard clucking at a school, and "Saram saeul ryoe" ('help me') when a chicken is heard in a situation of danger. When people are told that the song "All by Myself" sounds like "*Oppa mansae*" in Korean (meaning 'Let's say hurray for our big brother'), most people hear exactly "Oppa mansae," although the words in the original lyrics are totally different. Even worse, when people are told beforehand that the static noise of a music CD sounds like a ghost, most of them hear "I need blood."

This shows that our imprinted experiences control our language competency and, hence, we hear what we want to hear.

Of course there is the opposing opinion asserting that language controls our mind, not the other way around. There have been studies in which participants categorized colored cards in correspondence with the number of existing colors in their language. Other arguments also support that one's way of thinking is influenced by one's language. For example, Dr. Whorf, a well known linguist, presented the hypothesis of linguistic relativity by which a person's awareness, thought processes, and culture are all contained within their language, supporting the concept of language determining thought. George Orwell also portrays this concept well in his novel 1984 with the idea of a government creating a language known as 'Newspeak' to prevent alternative thinking in common people. Regulating verbal communication means regulating people's actions.

The cry of a pregnant cat sounds like a human baby cry

One of the biggest differences between humans and animals is verbal communication, and a relationship between individuals is basically initiated by verbal expression coming out of the individuals' language competency. Instead of arguing whether language rules thought or vice versa, it is most accurate to say that language and action are closely and inseparably related.

There are many issues in society caused by the way people speak. The Korean language, in particular, has a very delicate system of honorific forms in word endings that depend on age and social position. By not using proper honorific word endings or by using non-honorific imperative forms, people can hurt others, or even cause violence to arise. Very often, conflicts arise from our hearing what we want to hear and from our saying what we want to say without being considerate of others. Looking at our society today in which freedom of expression and aggressive usage of slang and profane words are popular, some of us may become reminiscent of the good old days and the government campaign in the 1960s and 70s that said, “Let's use nice words with others.” Indeed, to continue to hear others speak nicely, one should respond nicely in turn.

When people hear sounds, they usually use associated memories from previous experiences to figure out what the sounds are and it works for children, too

A few years ago, Anne Karpf, a British journalist, sociologist, and broadcaster, who has been researching the changes in the voices of British women for a long time, stated in her book *The Human Voice* that, along with the physical changes of increasing height and weight that are affecting women's voices, women have started to lower their voice tones in order to gain more recognition in a male-dominated society. Also, recently, the *English Daily Newspaper* reported that the movie *The Iron Lady*, a portrait of Margaret Thatcher's life, has once again revived a tendency in women to use low voices. This trend of women hoping to make their voices

Until recently, high-pitched and cheerful voices were thought representative of attractive women's voices (The scene of a heroine speaking in a high-pitched voice, taken from the movie *Madam Freedom* in 1956)

resemble Thatcher's low yet resolute tone of voice is called 'The Iron Lady Effect.' Furthermore, on the Internet, you can find many video clips of women making their voices extremely low and hoarse in what is called 'the vocal fry register.'

As a matter of fact, until recently, women's voices were known to be an octave higher than those of men; among women's voices, thin, high-pitched and cheerful voices were thought representative of women's voices. This way of thinking has been supported by research, published in Canada, in which men were more attracted to high-pitched voices in women and women were more attracted to low-pitched voices in men.

Of course, some believe that attractive voices may betray people. They think that if one person feels attracted to a voice, then others will also be attracted to the same voice, which will provide people of attractive voices with more chances of flirting with many people. Statistical research supports this belief, stating that men with low-pitched voices have more off-spring than other men, and that this is because women are unconsciously attracted to men with lower voices.

So, why would women give up their attractive high-pitched voices and try to speak in low-pitched voices?

Anne Karpf has two explanations for this phenomenon. Firstly, women have changed a lot physically. As women have become taller, the lengths of their vocal cords have also become longer, which has naturally lowered women's voices. Recent research has shown that the average voice of women

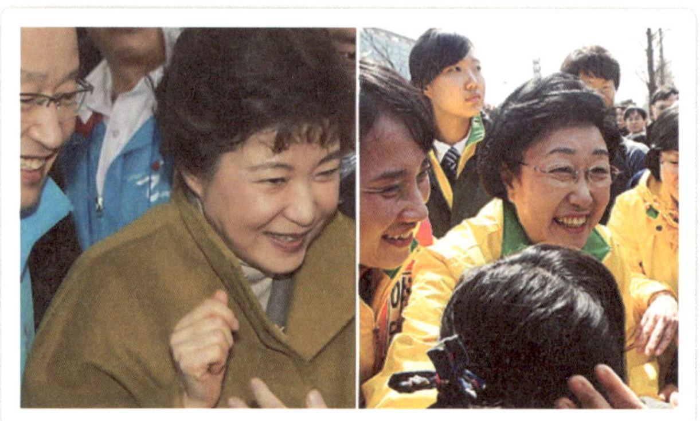

Unlike in the past when women passively followed behind men, women nowadays are equal to men in social and political status (Ms. Park, Keun-Hye and Ms. Han, Myung-Sook, well-known female politicians of Korea)

The trend of women hoping to make their voices resemble Thatcher's low yet resolute tone of voice is called "The Iron Lady Effect" (A scene from the movie *The Iron Lady*)

has lowered to about 2/3 of an octave higher than that of men, not an entire octave as was previously the case.

Nevertheless, as we can see in 'The Iron Lady Effect,' Karpf asserts that women's tendency to use low-pitched voices is a psychological phenomenon, which should be considered independent of physical changes. Unlike in the past when women passively followed behind men, women nowadays are equal to men in status. Consequently, women intentionally speak in low-pitched voices in order to avoid giving a weak impression to competitors and, in the long run, to gain more recognition.

Being more likely to win competitions if one has a lower-pitched voice can also be found in animal societies. For example, red deer, a typically polygamous species, use voice as a tool for competition. In order for a young red deer to challenge the leader of the herd, he has to first show off his strength through his cry. If the returning cry of the leader is lower than that of the challenger, then the challenger doesn't gain the chance to fight against the leader; however, if the pitches of the two are similar, the challenger will challenge the leader for his position.

It is true that there are many people who have a negative perspective of women who lower their voices in order to compete with men. This group of people completely deny the argument that a low-pitched voice represents strength. They insist that the strongest voice of all is the voice of the mother. There have been several studies to support their theory, and some of their major arguments are shown through the following results of studies on children: mothers' voices wake children up in the morning before any other sound; mothers' voices relieve stress in babies; and mothers' voices are the most effective tools for teaching languages to

Some people insist that the strongest voice of all is the voice of the mother waking children up in the morning before the children hear any other sound

children. In these studies, the pitch of mothers' voice was considered irrelevant; the voice itself had an enormous effect on children.

If you lower or thicken your voice below your normal voice range, it may hurt your vocal cords permanently. Besides, aging will stretch the vocal cord muscles and eventually produce a lower and thicker voice. You don't have to lower your voice intentionally since the time for having a lower voice will come to you soon enough.

From a linguistic as well as scientific point of view, speaking with more clarity and proper rhythm, instead of forcefully lowering the pitch of one's voice, should be recommended not only as a way to succeed in competition but also as a way to communicate effectively.